Grammar One

Teacher's Book

Kathryn Harper

Oxford University Press

Contents

Introduction

General

This book is a guide for teachers to **Grammar One** by Jennifer Seidl. It was written in consultation with her and is intended to help teachers make the best use of the student's book.

Grammar One is the first in a series of four grammar books designed to make grammar clear, interesting and easy to understand for young learners. All the books in the series follow basic coursebook syllabuses and are designed to be used alongside normal course work. The books can be worked through systematically or individual chapters can be selected in any order and used as needed.

Grammar One can be used by pre-teenagers and young teenagers in their first or second year of English language study. It has a communicative, activity-based approach to the learning of grammatical structures. One of the main features of the book is its variety and flexibility. It contains oral and written exercises as well as pairwork, classwork and individual work which can be used as the teacher sees fit.

Most of the material in the book revolves around the activities of an English family called the Bells, their friends, and an alien creature called Trig (from the planet Triglon). Trig is learning English. Trig's role in the book might be a comic one but its function is very serious. His struggles, frustrations and triumphs are a mirror of the pupils' own experience. Thus by becoming a figure of fun while learning English, Trig facilitates the learning process. The rest of the family functions as a reassuring, continuous presence, in particular the younger characters, Jenny and Nick, who are a similar age to the pupils.

Chapter structure of Grammar One

Each chapter of **Grammar One** contains the same elements, so that pupils will readily become familiar and comfortable with the book. Each chapter can take from twenty to forty-five minutes to complete, depending on how many of the optional activities and approaches the teacher decides to include.

Presentation   At the beginning of the chapter is a presentation section featuring an illustration and text (usually a dialogue) involving the characters. The presentation always introduces the grammar in context and some of the vocabulary.

Grammar lesson   The grammar lesson can be used by the teacher as a simplified guide to the structures covered. It often contains verb tables, general rules, examples and specific teaching points. The teacher need only direct pupils' attention to the grammar lesson if it fits into his or her own teaching plans and techniques.

Exercises   The exercises in this book have been designed so that they can be adapted to the needs of the individual teacher. Most exercises can be used in a number of ways: for write-in, oral, communicative, creative or activity based work. A great deal of care has been taken to make the exercise material relevant to the pupils' lives and interests.

How to use the teacher's book

The teacher's book offers advice on how best to exploit the material in the student's book. It also provides suggestions for additional activities to extend the exercises, the answers to the exercises, and tests (with an answer key).

Teaching aim This gives a clear indication of the structure (or structures) which will be covered in the chapter.

Vocabulary To help with lesson preparation, a selection of potentially difficult vocabulary is provided for pre-teaching. If a word has appeared in a previous chapter, it will not appear again.

Presentation In this section, there is advice on warm-up activities / questions, approaches to the presentation, things to point out to pupils, or tasks for pupils to carry out. The presentation section provides an opportunity to work on the pupils' oral expression and pronunciation. The presentation texts can be read several times by the teacher or the pupils and, since they introduce new structures, often require some explanation.

Grammar lesson This section contains ideas on how to best use the information contained in the grammar lesson box. The 'explanations' have been kept simple but can be easily supplemented with more information or examples.

It is often useful to read the presentation section with the pupils again, after completing the grammar lesson, in order to reinforce the structures covered.

Exercises There are various types of exercises and different ways in which they can be completed. At the beginning of the notes on each exercise, is an indication of whether it is oral or written, and if it is to be carried out as an individual, partner or class activity. The aim of each exercise is also supplied so that the structure being covered can be immediately identified. The rest of the notes provide advice on how to lead into the exercise, how the pupils are to do the exercise, any pitfalls which should be avoided and any material which ought to be reviewed before starting the exercise. Naturally, these are not hard and fast rules; each teacher should carry out an exercise in the way that works best for his or her class. However, since the exercises have been designed to give a balanced range of activities within a chapter, following these instructions will ensure that the important aspects of each structure are covered.

The section on additional activities suggests ways of extending the exercises for more practice. These activities often provide a complement to the exercise. They are sometimes creative activities which enable the pupils to express themselves within the limits of a grammatical structure.

Answers The answers to the exercises are given in a separate section within each chapter.

In cases where they can be short or long answers, the answers in the teacher's book reflect the example given in the student's book (this does not mean that the alternative answer is incorrect).

Where a choice of answers is possible, this is usually indicated.

Since many of the exercises are open-ended and dependent on the pupils' own responses, there is not always a complete list of answers. The pupils' responses should follow the example.

Tests

There are five tests at the end of the book which cover five chapters each. **These tests can be photocopied and used in class**. There is also a key for the tests.

1 Hello! I'm Jenny

Student's book pages 4 – 7

Teaching aims

- Subject pronouns: **I**, **you**, **he** etc.
- Present simple of **be**: **am**, **is**, **are**

Vocabulary

brother	pet	sister
dog	planet	visitor

Presentation

Tell pupils that they are going to read about an English family called the Bells. Show them the pictures of Jenny, Nick, their dog Chip and Trig, who is an alien from a planet called Triglon. Trig is learning to speak English

Read the presentation aloud to the pupils using the pictures to help explain the meaning.

Grammar lesson

Introduce subject pronouns. Use the pictures in the grammar lesson to show what they replace. Get pupils to practise replacing people and objects with pronouns. Ask pupils to find the subject pronouns in the presentation and use the pictures to show to whom they refer.

Introduce the present simple form of **be**. Look at the verb tables in the grammar lesson with the pupils and practise saying the different forms of **be**. Explain that the long forms and the short forms mean the same thing. Ask pupils to make their own sentences with **be**.

Read the presentation again. Pupils take turns reading and playing the different roles.

1 What's missing?

[written   individual]

Aim: subject pronouns with long and short forms of **be**

Pupils cover up the **be** table in the grammar lesson and look at the exercise. They write in the long form of **be** when the short form is provided and the short form of **be** when the long form is provided. If they can't remember all the forms, tell them to look at the **be** table. Remind them that both forms mean the same thing.

Pupils can read out their answers. Correct their pronunciation.

Additional activity: Do an oral drill by saying one form of **be** (long or short) and asking pupils to say the other. Use both affirmative and negative forms.

2 Hello!

[oral / written   individual]

Aim: present simple of **be** (long form)

a   Pupils complete the sentences by writing the correct form of **be** (**am**, **is**, or **are**) in the gaps.

b   Pupils take turns reading out their sentences. Correct their pronunciation.

Additional activity: Pupils write three sentences about themselves like those in the exercise, using the long form of **be**.

3 What's your name?

[oral / written   individual]

Aim: present simple of **be** (short form)

a   Tell pupils that Jenny is speaking. Pupils complete the sentences by writing the short forms of **be** in the gaps.

b   Pupils take turns reading out their sentences. Correct their pronunciation.

Additional activity: Pupils read out the sentences again, transforming the verbs into their long forms.

4 Change the sentences

[oral   class]

Aim: subject pronouns

Pupils take turns reading the sentences and replacing the names with **he**, **she**, **it**, or **they**. Correct their pronunciation.

Additional activities:
- The exercise is repeated but this time pupils close their books and the teacher or a pupil reads the prompts.
- Pupils write the sentences for homework.

5 Arrange the words

[written   individual]

Aims: subject pronouns and word order

Tell pupils that Trig is trying to make sentences with the blocks but he isn't getting them right. Ask pupils to look at the example showing Trig's incorrect sentence and the two correct ones. Remind pupils of the different parts of the sentence.

Pupils write sentences using the words in the blocks. The number in the blocks indicates its position in the sentence. (Every sentence must have a 1, 2 and 3 block.)

Additional activity: On a piece of paper, each pupil writes three of his own sentences (using nouns and pronouns). He cuts them into blocks (numbered 1, 2 and 3) and gives them to his partner to arrange in order. The partner reads out the sentences.

6 Friends

[oral   class]

Aims: subject pronouns and present simple of **be**

a Ask pupils to read about Nick and Jenny's friends. They look at the text and say what is the same about the characters.

b Remind pupils of how we make short answers. Pupils take turns reading the questions and answering them with short answers.

Additional activities:
- Pupils write the answers to **a** for homework.
- Pupils write five questions like those in **b** about themselves and their classmates. Their partners answer the questions.

Answers

1 What's missing?

1	he's	6	they are
2	I am	7	it is
3	she is not	8	I'm not
4	you aren't	9	he isn't
5	we aren't		

2 Hello!

1	is	7	is
2	is	8	is
3	are	9	are
4	am	10	is
5	is	11	is
6	are		

3 What's your name?

1	**I'm**	6	We**'re**
2	He**'s**	7	He**'s**
3	We**'re**	8	He **isn't**
4	He**'s**	9	He**'s**
5	**I'm**	10	He**'s**

4 Change the sentences

1. He isn't eleven.
2. It is near London.
3. He is twelve.
4. She isn't twelve.
5. They are brother and sister.
6. He is a good friend.
7. They are from Merton.
8. It is a small town.
9. He is a visitor from Triglon.
10. It is a small planet.
11. He is a good dog.
12. He is four years old.

5 Arrange the words

(Answers in any order)

Nick is twelve.
He is twelve.
Trig is from Triglon.
He is from Triglon.
Jenny is eleven.
She is eleven.
Nick is from Merton.
He is from Merton.
Nick and Jenny are from Merton.
They are from Merton.

6 Friends

a 1 George and Zoe are from Greece.
2 Zoe and Maria are thirteen.
3 Nick and Jenny are from England.
4 Nick and Carlo are twelve.
5 Jenny and George are eleven.

b 1 Yes, he is.
2 No, he isn't.
3 No, they aren't.
4 Yes, she is.
5 Yes, they are.
6 Yes, they are.
7 Yes, he is.
8 Yes, they are.
9 Yes, she is.
10 No, he isn't.
11 No, she isn't.
12 Yes, he is.
13 Yes, they are.
14 Yes, she is.
15 No, she isn't.
16 No, they aren't.
17 No, he isn't.

(18, 19, 20 – pupils' own answers)

2 A big book for Trig

Student's book pages 8 – 11

Teaching aims

- Articles: **a/an**, **the**
- Position of adjectives
- Nationality adjectives

Vocabulary

aeroplane	coin	letter	spoon
banknote	dictionary	passport	umbrella
basket	flag	plate	

Presentation

Tell pupils that Jenny and Nick have got two books for Trig. Read the presentation aloud and use the illustrations to make sure that pupils understand the text.

Grammar lesson

Write **a** and **an** on the board. Review vowels and consonants. Look at the examples in the grammar lesson. Ask pupils to say them and write them under **a** or **an** on the board. Ask pupils for other nouns (or adjective/noun combinations) and write them in the **a** or **an** list.

Rub out **a** and **an** and write **the** on the board. Pupils say all the words on the board with **the**.

Look at the examples of the position of adjectives in the grammar lesson. Ask pupils to give you other examples. Write them on the board.

Write the countries in the grammar lesson on the board and ask pupils how to describe a person who comes from these countries (using a nationality adjective). Write the correct answers on the board and stress the need for a capital letter. Point out that some of these words are also the languages spoken in the countries. Tell pupils to learn the list by heart.

1 What's in the picnic basket?

[oral/written   individual/class]

Aim: **a** or **an**

Ask pupils to look at the picture. Make sure that they know the English names of everything in the basket. Pupils write the words in the correct column with **a** or **an**. You can ask them to read out their lists. Correct their pronunciation.

Additional activity: Help pupils make a list of foods you can take on a picnic. Write the words on the board under **a** or **an**. Ask each pupil to write his three favourite foods to take on a picnic with **a** or **an**. Each pupil reads his favourites to the class.

2 Guess the words

[written   individual]

Aim: **a** or **an**

Tell pupils that each ∗ represents a missing letter. Remind them that when they see **an** it is a hint that the word must begin with a vowel (review vowels if necessary). Pupils write out the complete words in the spaces provided.

Additional activity: Divide the class into three or four groups. Each group writes a list of five words with letters missing like the ones in the exercise (with **a** or **an**). The other groups must guess what the words are.

3 Memory game

[oral   partner/class]

Aims: **a** or **an** and **the**

a Make sure that pupils know the English names of all the objects on the table in the picture. Pupils look at the picture for one minute. They close their books and name all the objects using **a** or **an** correctly. This can be done by the whole class together or in pairs, with one partner naming the objects and the other one checking to see if he's right.

b Same as above, except that pupils name the objects with **the**. Pupils might only need a few seconds to look at the picture this time.

Additional activity: One pupil closes his eyes and his partner gives him different objects to identify by touch. The first pupil must guess what they are using **a** or **an**.

4 Get it right

[written   individual]

Aims: word order and position of adjectives

Tell pupils that the words are not in the right order. Pupils put them in order and write correct sentences. They may need to be reminded about the order of adjectives in a sentence. Pupils can read out their sentences.

Additional activity: Pupils look at their answers and make new sentences by changing the adjectives. They read the sentences to the class.
▶ Trig is a special friend.
  Trig is a good friend.

5 What are they?

[oral / written   individual]

Aim: nationality adjectives

Review nationality adjectives with the aid of a map of the world if you have one. Pupils look at the pictures and say the correct nationality adjective for the objects with **a** or **an**. Do this orally at first to review difficult vocabulary and then get pupils to write in the answers in class or at home. Make sure they don't forget to capitalize the first letters.

Additional activity: Pupils cover their answers and, in pairs, ask and answer questions about the things.
▶ PUPIL 1 *Is it an Italian stamp?*
  PUPIL 2 *Yes, it is.* (OR *No, it isn't.*)

Answers

1 What's in the picnic basket?

(Answers in any order)

a	**an**
a plate	an apple
a sandwich	an ice-cream
a spoon	an orange

2 Guess the words

1	an arm	9	an egg
2	a sister	10	a bicycle
3	a lesson	11	a basket
4	a school	12	a football
5	an umbrella	13	an animal
6	a father	14	a book
7	an orange	15	an exercise
8	an apple	16	a letter

3 Memory game

(Answers in any order)

a
an envelope	a pencil
an exercise book	a pen
an atlas	a ruler
an aeroplane	a glass
an elephant	a dictionary (OR
an apple	an English dictionary)
	a lamp

b
the envelope	the pencil
the exercise book	the pen
the atlas	the ruler
the aeroplane	the glass
the elephant	the dictionary (OR
the apple	the English dictionary)
	the lamp

4 Get it right

1 Trig is a special friend.
2 Triglon is not a big planet.
3 Merton is a small town.
4 The grammar book is not big.
5 The dictionary is very thick.
6 Nick and Jenny are English.
7 Carlo and Maria are Italian.
8 Dimitris is a Greek name.
9 Carlo is an Italian name.
10 Trig is not an English name.

5 What are they?

1	an American	7	a French
2	a Greek	8	a Turkish
3	a Spanish	9	a German
4	an English	10	an Italian
5	an American	11	an Egyptian
6	an Italian	12	a Greek

3 Girls and boys

Student's book pages 12 – 13

Teaching aims

- Regular and irregular plurals
- Pronunciation of plurals

Vocabulary

bench	melon	policeman
bush	peach	radish

Presentation

Ask pupils to look at the picture. Ask them to say who is in the picture (a man, a woman, etc.). Write the words on the board. Ask pupils to say the plural forms for the words on the board. Read the text aloud to the class.

Grammar lesson

Tell pupils that there are different ways to form the plural of nouns. Use the table in the grammar lesson to show the different ways in which the regular plural of nouns is made. Ask pupils to give other examples and write them on the board.

Demonstrate the pronunciation of the various forms and practice it with the pupils. Make sure they recognize the difference between the **s** and **z** sounds.

Tell the pupils that some nouns have irregular plurals. Read the examples in the grammar lesson. Tell pupils that they must learn these. Pupils use them in sentences.

1 Making lists

[oral / written   individual]

Aim: plural of nouns (form and pronunciation)

a Read through the words to make sure pupils understand them. At the top of the empty lists are indications of how the nouns are made plural. Pupils put the words in the correct lists, writing them in plural form.

b Pupils read out the lists. Correct their pronunciation.

Additional activity: Ask pupils to suggest more singular nouns, write them on the board and ask pupils which list they belong to.

2 At the market

[oral / written   individual]

Aim: plural of nouns (form and pronunciation)

Ask pupils what fruits and vegetables you find on a fruit and vegetable stall. Look at the picture. Make sure pupils are familiar with the different fruits and vegetables in the picture.

Pupils write in the endings and then take turns reading out the words. Correct their pronunciation.

Additional activity: With the pupils, make a list of fruits and vegetables not found in the picture. Pupils write their plural forms.

3 Word square

[oral / written   individual]

Aim: plural of nouns (form)

Ask pupils to look at the examples in the word square and read them out. Pupils circle all the plural words in the same way. The words can be found in a horizontal or vertical position. Once they have circled as many as they can, ask them how many they have found (they should include the examples). Pupils read out the words. Correct their pronunciation.

Additional activity: Dictate the words from the word square to the pupils. Check their spelling.

4 In the park

[written   individual]

Aim: plural of nouns

Tell pupils that the two pictures are similar but not the same. They must find out what is different. Pupils look at the pictures and write down what they can see in each one. Sometimes the nouns will be singular and sometimes they will be plural.

Additional activity: Pupils draw their own simplified versions of 'spot the difference' pictures like these and their partners say what there is in each picture.

Answers

1 Making lists

(Answers in any order)

s	es	ies
roads	boxes	stories
pens	tomatoes	countries
friends	beaches	cities
shirts	buses	babies
boys	bushes	parties
cars	benches	dictionaries
desks	watches	**Irregular**
girls	matches	feet
trees	dishes	women
days	glasses	children
dogs	potatoes	people
		policemen

2 At the market

(Answers in any order)

potatoes	figs
radishes	strawberries
oranges	cherries
dates	peaches
lemons	melons
bananas	tomatoes

3 Word square

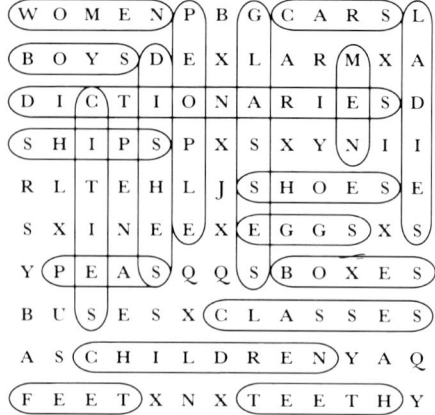

(Answers in any order)

There are twenty words (including the examples).

► women
► dishes

cars	peas	teeth
boys	boxes	cities
dictionaries	buses	people
ships	classes	glasses
shoes	children	men
eggs	feet	ladies

4 In the park

Picture A	Picture B
1 one child	11 three children
2 two babies	12 one baby
3 one man	13 two men
4 one dog	14 two dogs
5 three birds	15 one bird
6 two bushes	16 one bush
7 one bus	17 two buses
8 two benches	18 one bench
9 one tree	19 three trees
10 two clouds	20 one cloud

4 Meet my teacher

Teaching aim

- Possessive adjectives: **my**, **your**, **his**, **her** etc.

Vocabulary

basketball	chicken	fair	steak
beefburgers	dark	singer	swimming

Presentation

Explain that Nick and Jenny are talking about their school and their friends. Ask some pupils to read the presentation aloud. Point out the words in thick type and ask pupils what they mean. Use the pictures to explain relationships of possession.

Grammar lesson

Review subject pronouns (see Chapter 1). Look at the table in the grammar lesson with pupils and show them how possessive adjectives relate to pronouns. Explain the use of possessive adjectives and look at the examples with the class. Point out the difference between **its** (possession) and **it's** (it is).

Pupils practise the form by saying the correct possessive adjective when given a pronoun. Indicate objects in the class belonging to people and ask pupils to identify them with **my**, **her**, **his**, **their**, **our**.

Ask some of the pupils to read the presentation aloud again.

1 Her name is ...

[oral / written   individual]

Aim: **your**, **his**, **her**, **its** and **their**

Pupils read the text to themselves and write **your**, **his**, **her**, **its** or **their** in the gaps. Then they read out their answers. Correct their pronunciation.

Additional activity: Pupils write the answers to the questions in the last paragraph in full sentences.

2 Favourites

[oral   individual / class]

Aim: **her**, **his**, **their** and **my**

Look at the table with the pupils and explain that it is about the Bells' favourites. Explain the different categories. Pupils fill in the **You** column with their own favourites. They say sentences about the table as shown in the example (with **her**, **his**, **their** or **my**).

Additional activities:
- Pupils write out the answers for homework.
- Pupils make their own tables. They ask two or three other pupils questions about their favourites with **your**. They tell the class what they have found out.

3 Guessing game

[oral   class]

Aim: **her** and **his**

A pupil chooses one of the characters on the page and his classmates must identify the character by asking questions with **her** or **his** (as in the example). The questions are about the characters' appearances and favourites (which are listed). Make sure pupils use possessive pronouns correctly.

Additional activities:
- Pupils choose three or four of the characters and write descriptions of them.
  - ▶ Mary
  Her hair is short and dark. Her favourite sport is swimming. Her favourite food is pizza. Her favourite colour is blue.
- Pupils write descriptions of three or four of their classmates.

4 Ask your partner

[oral   partner]

Aim: **your** and **my**

Tell pupils that they must talk about favourites again. Read the example and look at the topics with pupils. Add others if necessary. With their partners, pupils ask and answer ten questions.

Additional activity: Pupils tell the class what they have found out about their partners using **his** or **her**.
- ▶ *His favourite colour is orange.*

Answers

1 Her name is . . .

1	Their	10	their
2	Her	11	Its
3	Her	12	Her
4	Her	13	His
5	His	14	your
6	Their OR	15	your
	His	16	its
7	His	17	your
8	his	18	their
9	Their		

2 Favourites

Jenny
Her favourite sport is swimming.
Her favourite food is chocolate cake.

Nick
His favourite music is rock.
His favourite singer is Sting.
His favourite sport is football.
His favourite food is ice-cream.

Mr and Mrs Bell
Their favourite music is opera.
Their favourite singer is Pavarotti.
Their favourite sport is tennis.
Their favourite food is pizza.

3 Guessing game

No fixed answers. Follow example.

PUPIL	*It's a girl.*
CLASS	*Is her hair dark?*
PUPIL	*Yes, it is.*
CLASS	*Is her hair long?*
PUPIL	*No, it isn't.*
CLASS	*Is her favourite colour red?*
PUPIL	*No, it isn't.*
CLASS	*Is it Kate?*
PUPIL	*Yes, it is!*

4 Ask your partner

Pupils' own answers. Follow example.

PUPIL 1	*What is your favourite colour?*
PUPIL 2	*My favourite colour is orange.*

5 Is it Nick's?

Teaching aim

- Possessives ('s and s')
  (see Chapter 4 for possessive adjectives)

Vocabulary

aunt   neighbour   skateboard   Walkman
daughter   pen-friend   uncle

Presentation

Ask pupils to look at the pictures. Read the text to the pupils and use the pictures to emphasize the idea of possession. Ask pupils to guess who owns what.

Grammar lesson

Read through the examples in the grammar lesson with the pupils and show how possessives are formed with singular and plural (regular and irregular) nouns. Point out the position of the apostrophe changes with the different forms. Ask pupils for more examples of irregular plurals and write their possessive forms on the board.

Explain the difference between **'s** for possession and **'s** for **is**. Tell pupils that a good way of finding out the meaning of **'s** is to try to replace it with **is** (long form).

1 Nick talks about his pictures

[written   individual]

Aim: possessive or short form of **is**

Tell pupils that Nick is talking about his pictures. Ask them to look at the pictures and read the text aloud. Explain any of the text they don't understand. The pupils pick out the words with apostrophes and put them into the **Possessives** or the **Short forms** list.

Additional activity: Pupils ask each other questions about the things or people in the pictures.
- ▶ PUPIL 1   *Is it the Todds' house?*
  PUPIL 2   *Yes, it is the Todds' house.* OR
  No, it's the Allens' house.

2 Who are they?

[oral / written   individual]

Aim: possessives

Review the words **father, mother, daughter, sister, brother, children, friend**. Using the word in brackets as a prompt, pupils say and then write sentences about the relationships between the characters in the book. Even if they cannot remember the relationships between all the characters, they should still try to get the form right.

Additional activity: Pupils transform the sentences they have written into questions and say them.
- ▶ Mrs Allen is Tom's mother.
  Is Mrs Allen Tom's mother?

3 Names

[written   individual]

Aim: possessives

Review relationships again if necessary. Remind pupils about plural forms. Pupils make sentences about the names of different people they know. Encourage them to use the long form as opposed to the short form of **be** (less confusing). Pupils write down their answers.

Not all the questions will be appropriate for every pupil (they might not have a pet etc.). If this is the case, they can invent an answer.

Additional activity: Pupils read their sentences to the class.

Answers

1 Nick talks about his pictures

(Answers in any order)

Possessives	Short forms
Tom's	Walkman's
Mr Allen's	name's
Tom's	Amanda's
Jenny's	bicycle's
Todds'	
Amanda's	
Chip's	
Todds'	

2 Who are they?

1. Mrs Todd is Amanda's mother.
2. Mr Allen is Tom's father.
3. Mr Blake is Nick's teacher.
4. Amanda is Mr and Mrs Todd's daughter.
5. Jenny is Nick's sister.
6. Mr Todd is Amanda's father.
7. Chip is the Bells' dog.
8. Trig is the children's friend.
9. Amanda is Jenny's best friend.
10. Miss Mill is Jenny's teacher.
11. Tom is Nick's best friend.
12. Jenny and Nick are Mr and Mrs Bell's children.

3 Names

Pupils' own answers.

1. My English teacher's name is . . .
2. My brother's name is . . . OR
   My brothers' names are . . .
3. My best friend's name is . . . OR
   My best friends' names are . . .
4. My father's name is . . .
5. My mother's name is . . .
6. My uncle's name is . . . OR
   My uncles' names are . . .
7. My aunt's name is . . . OR
   My aunts' names are . . .
8. My cousin's name is . . . OR
   My cousins' names are . . .
9. My doctor's name is . . .
10. My pen-friend's name is . . .
11. My pet's name is . . . OR
    My pets' names are . . .
12. My neighbour's name is . . . OR
    My neighbours' names are . . .

6 What have the Bells got?

Student's book pages 18 – 19

Teaching aim

● Present simple of **have got**

Vocabulary

balloon	clock	penguin	sunroof	telescope
boat	gorilla	socks	sweater	watch

Presentation

Ask pupils to look at the picture of the car. Read the text aloud to them and explain any vocabulary they don't know. Ask pupils to find the different forms of **have got** in the text.

Grammar lesson

Introduce the forms of **have got**. Ask pupils to look at the verb table. Point out how the form changes with **he**, **she** or **it**. Practise long and short forms by reading out one and asking pupils to say the other. Look at the negative, question and short answer forms with pupils. Tell pupils that **got** is not used in short answers.

Ask pupils to make sentences about themselves, their houses or their families' cars with **have got**.

Ask a few pupils to read the presentation section aloud again.

1 What have you got?

[oral individual]

Aim: present simple of **have got** (with **I** and **we**)

Make sure pupils know the names of the objects in the picture. Pupils say fourteen sentences based on the examples. Each sentence must include one thing they (**I've**) or their families (**we've**) have got and another thing they or their families haven't got.

Additional activity: Pupils interview each other about what they have and haven't got using questions and short answers.

▶   PUPIL 1 *Have you got an island?*
    PUPIL 2 *Yes, I have.* OR *No, I haven't.*

2 What's in the school bags?

[oral individual/class]

Aim: present simple of **have got**

a Ask pupils to look at the first picture and say what Jenny has got in her school bag. Read out the example. Pupils look at the other pictures and say what the characters have and haven't got in their school bags. Each character has got four things and hasn't got one thing.

Pupils say which characters have got the same things.

b Ask pupils what other things they might have in their school bags. Write a list on the board. Pupils use the vocabulary from **a** or the new vocabulary to ask and answer questions about what five other pupils have in their school bags. If pupils haven't got school bags then ask what they have got in their pockets etc.

Additional activity: Pupils write the sentences from part **a** in class or for homework.

3 Partner game

[written individual/partner]

Aim: present simple of **have got** (affirmative, interrogative and short answer forms)

a Briefly review the position of adjectives and nouns in a sentence. Pupils look at the list of colours and things and read the example sentences. They make true sentences about what they have got, using a word from each list.

b In pairs, pupils try to guess what their partners have written by asking questions with **have got** and combinations of the words from the two lists. The partners reply with short answers.

Additional activity: Pupils report to the class what their partners have got.
▶   *John has got a blue sweater, a red pen . . .*

4 Look at Trig!

[oral class]

Aim: present simple of **have got** (interrogative and short answer forms)

Make sure pupils understand the words in the two lists. Pupils look at the picture of Trig. They take turns to ask and answer questions about him using the interrogative form of **has got** and short answers. They use a word from each list to make the questions.

Additional activity: Pupils use **have got** and the words in the lists to write true sentences about Trig.

▶ *Trig has got small ears.*

Answers

1 What have you got?

Pupils' own answers. Follow examples.

▶ *I've got a watch, but I haven't got a doll.*

▶ *We've got a cat, but we haven't got a dog.*

The possible things are:

a doll	a gorilla
a Walkman	a penguin
a car	a telescope
a cat	a spaceship
a clock	a dog
a bus	a fish / goldfish
a bicycle	an aeroplane / plane
a piano	a watch
a balloon	a television / TV
an island	a radio
a boat / ship	a tennis racket
a football	a camera

2 What's in the school bags?

a 1 Tom has got an exercise book, a paint box, a brush and a pencil.
He hasn't got an atlas.

2 Nick has got an atlas, an exercise book, a paint box and a pencil.
He hasn't got a brush.

3 Carlo has got an atlas, a paint box, a pencil and a brush.
He hasn't got an exercise book.

4 Amanda has got an exercise book, an atlas, a pencil and a brush.
She hasn't got a paint box.

5 Maria has got an atlas, an exercise book, a brush and a pencil.
She hasn't got a paint box.

6 Zoe has got an atlas, an exercise book, a pencil and a brush.
She hasn't got a paint box.

Zoe and Maria have got the same things.
Jenny and Carlo have got the same things.

b Pupils' own answers. Follow example.
▶ PUPIL 1 *Have you got a pencil?*
PUPIL 2 *Yes, I have.* OR *No, I haven't.*

3 Partner game

a Pupils' own answers. Follow examples.
▶ *I've got a green sweater.*
▶ *I've got a red T-shirt.*
Any colour can go with any thing.

b Pupils' own answers. Follow example.
▶ PUPIL 1 *Have you got a white sweater?*
PUPIL 2 *No, I haven't.*
PUPIL 1 *Have you got a green sweater?*
PUPIL 2 *Yes, I have.*

4 Look at Trig!

Pupils' own answers. Follow example.
▶ PUPIL *Has he got a fat body?*
CLASS *Yes, he has.*

7 These are mine

Teaching aims

- Demonstratives: **this** / **these**, **that** / **those**
- Possessive pronouns: **mine**, **yours**, **his**, **hers** etc.

Vocabulary

boots	garden	milk-shake
cap	glove	snack
cassette	jacket	socks

Presentation

Tell pupils that Nick and Jenny can't decide who the cassettes belong to. Read the text to the pupils. Use the pictures to show the difference in distance between **this** / **these** and **that** / **those**. Explain what **mine** and **yours** means.

Ask two pupils to read the text using gestures to illustrate **this** / **these**, **that** / **those** and **mine** / **yours**.

Grammar lesson

Use the table and the illustrations in the grammar lesson to explain the form and use of demonstratives.

Review possessive adjectives with pupils (form and use). Use the table to explain how possessive pronouns replace possessive adjectives and nouns. Tell pupils to learn the list by heart.

Ask pupils to make sentences about objects in the classroom using demonstratives and possessive pronouns.

1 These and those

[oral   individual]

Aim: **this** / **these** and **that** / **those**

Ask pupils to explain when we use **this is** / **there are** and **that is** / **those are**. Point out that expressions like **here** or **over there** indicate whether something is near or far. Tell pupils to pay attention to plurals and singulars. Pupils read the sentences and cross out the incorrect forms. They can take turns to read the correct sentences out to the class.

Additional activity: Pupils read out the sentences again, replacing possessive adjectives and nouns with possessive pronouns.

▶ This is my orange juice.
  This is mine.

2 This exercise . . .

[oral / written   individual / class]

Aim: **this is** or **these are**

Pupils look at the sentences and identify the objects as singular or plural. They say the correct demonstrative with **be**. Then they write it in.

Additional activity: Pupils must imagine that the objects are far away and read the sentences again, putting in **that is** or **those are**.

3 Missing words

[written   individual]

Aim: possessive pronouns (form)

Pupils cover the grammar lesson. They look at the table and write in the missing words. Explain that the first column is for subject pronouns, the second column is for possessive adjectives and the third column is for possessive pronouns.

Additional activity: One pupil closes his book and his partner reads out the subject pronouns. The pupil must say the possessive adjectives and possessive pronouns which correspond to the subject pronouns.

4 His, hers or theirs?

[written   individual]

Aim: possessive pronouns

Pupils read the questions then look at Exercise 2 for the answers. They write in the answers using possessive pronouns.

Additional activity: Pupils write three questions of their own about Exercise 2. They ask their partners who must answer correctly.

▶ PUPIL 1   *Is the scarf Mr Bell's?*
  PUPIL 2   *No, it's not his.*

Answers

1 These and those

1 Those are our beefburgers over there.
2 This is Jenny's cheeseburger.
3 This is your Coke here.
4 These are Tom's ice-creams.
5 That's Amanda's chocolate cake.
6 That's Chip's bone in the garden.
7 Those are her crisps over there.
8 That's Nick's lemonade.
9 This is Jenny's ice-lolly.
10 And those are Trig's three giant milk-shakes over there!

2 This exercise . . .

1 These are, this is
2 This is, these are
3 This is, this is
4 These are, these are
5 This is, these are

3 Missing words

1	your	2	yours
3	he	4	his
5	her	6	hers
7	our	8	ours
9	you	10	yours
11	their	12	theirs

4 His, hers or theirs?

1 Yes, it's his.
2 No, they aren't hers.
3 Yes, they're theirs.
4 No, it isn't his.
5 Yes, they're theirs.
6 Yes, it's hers.
7 No, they aren't his.

8 A picnic

Student's book pages 22–23

Teaching aim

- Countable and uncountable nouns with **a/an** or **some**
  (see Chapter 19 for countables and uncountables with **some**, **any**, **how much** and **how many**)

Vocabulary

cherries	crisps	jam	sandwich
chips	eggs	orange juice	sweets

(Please note that **ice-cream** is treated as a countable noun in this book but it can also be uncountable. **Chocolate** is treated as an uncountable here but can also be countable.)

Presentation

Tell pupils that Nick, Jenny and Amanda are having a picnic and they have all brought different things to eat. Ask pupils to read the text. Ask pupils to identify the different food items in the picture.

Read the text again with pupils pointing out that sometimes you say **a** or **an** and sometimes you say **some** before a noun.

Grammar lesson

Write a list of the countable nouns from the presentation on the board (**banana**, **orange**, **biscuit**, **crisp**) in singular form. Show how they are used with **a** (or **an**). Ask pupils to say their plural forms and write them in another list on the board with **some**.

Now write a list of the uncountable nouns from the presentation on the board with **some**. Explain that singular verbs are used with uncountable nouns.

Ask pupils to make their own sentences with countable and uncountable nouns.

1 A picnic

[written   individual]

Aim: **a/an** or **some** with countable and uncountable nouns

Review the vocabulary. Pupils identify whether the nouns are countable or uncountable, singular or plural and write in **a**, **an** or **some**. They can read out their answers to the class.

Additional activity: One pupil says a noun from the exercise as a prompt. His partner must repeat it with **a**, **an** or **some**. Pupils can also do this with nouns other than those in the exercise.

- PUPIL 1   *milk-shake*
  PUPIL 2   *a milk-shake*

2 Right or wrong?

[oral   individual]

Aim: **a/an** or **some** with countable and uncountable nouns

Ask pupils to look at the pictures. Make sure they know the vocabulary. Tell pupils that some of the food is not linked to the right word. Only singular countable nouns should be matched up to **a/an**. Plural countables and uncountables should be matched up to **some**. Pupils write a ✔ in the boxes where they are correctly matched up and a ✗ where they are incorrectly matched up. They say the correct answers.

Additional activity: Pupils write out the words with **a**, **an** or **some**.

3 What have they got?

[written individual]

Aim: **a / an** or **some** with countable and uncountable nouns

Explain to pupils that each character is joined to two or more food items. Show them the example. Pupils look at the maze in order to write the correct words with **a**, **an** or **some** in the gaps. They can read out their answers to the class.

Additional activity: With the help of the class, write other countable and uncountable food items (such as fruits and vegetables from Chapter 3, Exercise 2) on the board. In their books, pupils replace the food in the maze with some of these and do the exercise again orally.

Answers

1 A picnic

1	some	7	an
2	some	8	some
3	a	9	a
4	some	10	some
5	some	11	some
6	some	12	an

2 Right or wrong?

1 ✗ some lemonade
2 ✓ an orange
3 ✗ some Coke
4 ✗ some sugar
5 ✗ some bread
6 ✓ an egg
7 ✓ some grapes
8 ✓ some flour
9 ✗ a banana
10 ✓ some milk
11 ✗ a sandwich
12 ✓ some apples

3 What have they got?

(Order of answers can vary within each sentence.)

Nick's got 1 an ice-cream and 2 some biscuits.
Amanda's got 3 some chocolate and 4 some cheese.
Miss Mill's got 5 some biscuits and 6 a banana.
Tom's got 7 an ice-cream and 8 a banana.
Mr Blake's got 9 some chocolate and 10 an apple.
Trig's got 11 some cheese, 12 an apple, 13 a banana, 14 an ice-cream, 15 some chocolate and 16 some biscuits.

9 I like school

Teaching aim

- Present simple with **I**, **you**, **we** and **they**
  (see Chapter 10 for the present simple with **he**, **she**
  and **it**; see Chapters 11 and 12 for question forms)

Vocabulary

breakfast	get up	guitar	riding
comics	ground	hobby	stickers
dinner	grow	lunch	wear

It would be a good idea to review time and numbers
before starting this chapter.

Presentation

Ask pupils what they do every day. Ask them what they
think Nick and Jenny do every day. Read the text to
them. Write the verbs on the board and explain their
meaning.

Grammar lesson

Explain the verb table to the pupils. Ask them to repeat **I**,
you, **we** and **they** with **like** (affirmative and negative
forms). Ask them to do the same thing with the verbs
from the presentation. Explain the three uses of the
present simple described here and ask pupils to look at
the examples.

Ask pupils to make sentences about themselves in the
present simple.

1 Jenny and Nick's day

[oral / written   individual]

Aim: present simple with **they**

Tell pupils that this exercise is about what Nick and
Jenny do every day. Remind them that **they** replaces two
or more people or things. Pupils cover up the
presentation. They say the correct answers then write
them down in class or for homework.

Additional activity: Pupils close their books and say
five things that Nick and Jenny do every day.

2 Your day

[oral   individual / class]

Aim: present simple with **I**

Tell pupils to read the sentences about Jenny and Nick
and transform them into sentences about themselves with
I. When their activities are the same as Nick and Jenny's
they add **too** to the end of the sentence.

Additional activities:
- Pupils write out their sentences for homework.
- When the pupils' sentences are different from Nick
  and Jenny's they write them down in the negative.
  - Nick and Jenny get up at seven thirty.
    I don't get up at seven thirty.

3 Nick's class

[oral   individual]

Aim: present simple with **they** and **I**

a   Tell pupils that this table is about Nick's class. The first
column is the list of subjects. The second column tells
them how many pupils like each subject. The third
column tells them how many pupils don't like each
subject. Pupils say sentences about the table as in the
example.

b   Pupils take turns to say which subjects they like and don't
like.

Additional activity: Ask pupils to help you make a
similar table about the class on the board. Pupils say or
write sentences about it as in **a**.

4 Hobbies and interests

[oral   class]

Aim: present simple with **I**

Explain the meaning of any of the hobbies and interests
which pupils do not know. Pupils say if they do or don't
do the hobby as shown in the examples.

Additional activity: Pupils write the answers in class
or for homework.

5 Nature quiz

[written   indiviudal]

Aim: present simple with **they**

Tell pupils that this exercise tests what they know about nature. Explain that the sentences are not true and that they must correct them as shown in the example. They will find parts of the answers at the bottom of the page. You might need to read over the sentences carefully to make sure pupils understand them before they do the exercise.

Additional activity: Pupils write five new sentences containing general facts about animals or nature. They read them to the class.

Answers

1 Jenny and Nick's day

1	have	6	play
2	walk	7	go
3	start	8	do
4	have	9	watch
5	do	10	go

2 Your day

Pupils' own answers.

1 I have breakfast at . . .
2 I . . . to school.
3 My lessons start at . . .
4 I work from . . . to . . .
5 I have lunch at . . .
6 I . . . in the afternoon.
7 I go home at . . .
8 I do my homework . . .
9 After dinner I . . .
10 I go to bed at . . .
11 I . . . in bed.
12 I go to sleep at . . .

3 Nick's class

a 1 Fourteen pupils like English and six pupils don't like English.
2 Eleven pupils like Geography and nine pupils don't like Geography.
3 Twelve pupils like History and eight pupils don't like History.
4 Ten pupils like Science and ten pupils don't like Science.
5 Eighteen pupils like Games and two pupils don't like Games.
6 Thirteen pupils like Music and seven pupils don't like Music.
7 Sixteen pupils like Art and four pupils don't like Art.

b Pupils' own answers. Follow example.
   ▶ *I like English but I don't like History.*

4 Hobbies and interests

1 I read books. O R I don't read books.
2 I watch television. O R I don't watch television.
3 I read comics. O R I don't read comics.
4 I listen to the radio. O R I don't listen to the radio.
5 I collect stamps. O R I don't collect stamps.
6 I play the piano. O R I don't play the piano.
7 I play football. O R I don't play football.
8 I go swimming. O R I don't go swimming.
9 I read newspapers. O R I don't read newspapers.
10 I collect posters. O R I don't collect posters.
11 I collect stickers. O R I don't collect stickers.
12 I play the guitar. O R I don't play the guitar.
13 I listen to music. O R I don't listen to music.
14 I play basketball. O R I don't play basketball.
15 I go riding. O R I don't go riding.
16 I play tennis. O R I don't play tennis.

5 Nature quiz

1 Wrong. Pandas don't live in Africa. They live in China.
2 Wrong. Fish don't swim in the air. They swim under water.
3 Wrong. Bananas don't grow in cold countries. They grow in hot countries.
4 Wrong. Kangaroos don't live in India. They live in Australia.
5 Wrong. Peanuts don't grow on trees. They grow in the ground.
6 Wrong. Penguins don't live at the North Pole. They live at the South Pole.
7 Wrong. Koalas don't eat fish. They eat leaves.

10 Chip likes ice-creams

Student's book pages 26–27

Teaching aim

- Present simple with **he**, **she** and **it**
  (see Chapter 9 for the present simple with **I**, **you**, **we**
  and **they**; see Chapters 11 and 12 for question forms)

Vocabulary

bath[n]	chase	peach	spinach
bone	chew	plum	steak
bury	flowerbed	smelly	tear[vb]

Presentation

Tell pupils to look at the picture of Chip and say what he
does every day and what he likes. Ask one or two pupils
to read the text aloud. Explain anything they do not
know.

Grammar lesson

Review the present simple with **I**, **you**, **we** and **they** by
asking the pupils what they, their friends, their families
etc. do every day and what they like. Write two of the
sentences on the board to use as examples.

Introduce the present simple with **he**, **she** and **it** by
writing one or two of the sentences from the presentation
on the board and comparing them with the **I**, **you**, **we**,
they sentences.

Pupils look at the grammar lesson and practise making
verb forms with **he**, **she** or **it** (substitute **like** with other
verbs). Remind them not to forget the **s**. Point out that
do changes to **does** with **he**, **she** and **it**.

1 Make lists

[written   individual]

Aim: present simple with **he**, **she** and **it**

Remind pupils of the three ways of writing the present
simple with **he**, **she** and **it**: **s**, **es**, **ies**. Pupils write each
word in the third person singular form in the correct list.
Pupils can take turns reading out their answers. Correct
their pronunciation.

Additional activity: Pupils close their books and write
three verbs for each ending (**s**, **es** or **ies**). They read out
their answers.

2 Daily timetable

[oral/written   partner]

Aim: present simple with **he/she**.

Pupils fill in the timetable giving true information about
what they do each day. They exchange books with their
partners. Each pupil reads out the information from his
partner's timetable, transforming the verbs into the third
person form. Make sure the **s** endings are clearly
pronounced.

Pupils can say the proper names of their partners instead
of the pronouns **he/she**.

Additional activity: Pupils write out the sentences for
homework.

3 Chip likes to help

[written   individual]

Aim: present simple with **he**

Pupils write the verbs which are on the left in the correct
form in each sentence. They can take turns to read out
the completed sentences.

Additional activities:
- Each pupil takes a piece of paper and draws a picture
  of one thing Chip does. He shows it to the class and
  the class finds the correct sentence in the exercise.
- One pupil mimes what Chip does while another pupil
  reads the text.

4 Food

[oral   individual]

Aim: present simple with **he**, **she** and **it**

Tell pupils that they're going to talk about the food Jenny, Nick, Trig and Chip like and don't like. Explain the table to the pupils: the ✔ means they like the food and the ✕ means they don't like it. Pupils say sentences, based on the example, about what the characters like and don't like.

Additional activities:
- Pupils write the answers for homework.
- Pupils make up their own charts with their own food categories and interview four other pupils. They read out what they have found.

5 Class game

[class   oral]

Aim: present simple with **I** and **he/she**

Ask pupils to name things they don't like (not only food). Write the more difficult words on the board. One pupil starts the game by saying one thing he doesn't like. The pupil next to him says what the first pupil doesn't like and adds what he doesn't like. Each pupil must repeat what the others before him have said then add what he dislikes. Make sure pupils transform the verbs correctly. When a pupil gets an answer wrong (form or content) the game begins again.

The game can be played several times but the pupils should change their answers each time.

Additional activities:
- Substitute **don't like** with **like** and play the game again.
- Use other verbs like *play* (a game or an instrument) or *learn* (a language, an activity, a subject at school) and play the game as before.

Answers

1 Make lists

s	es	ies
sees	washes	tries
buys	misses	buries
walks	mixes	hurries
learns	goes	cries
says	does	dries
starts	teaches	fries
comes	fixes	

2 Daily timetable

Pupils' own answers.

He/She eats breakfast at ...
He/She goes to school at ...
He/She leaves school at ...
He/She eats lunch at ...
He/She does his/her homework at ...
He/She eats dinner at ...
He/She watches television at ...
He/She goes to bed at ...
He/She falls asleep at ...

3 Chips likes to help

1	wakes	9	catches
2	barks	10	goes
3	makes	11	carries
4	doesn't	12	likes
5	tears	13	chews
6	digs	14	sees
7	buries	15	drops
8	chases	16	runs
		17	loves

4 Food

Jenny likes carrots, but she doesn't like spinach.
Nick likes spinach, but he doesn't like carrots.
Trig likes carrots and spinach.
Chip doesn't like carrots or spinach.
Jenny likes milk-shakes and fizzy drinks.
Nick likes fizzy drinks, but he doesn't like milk-shakes.
Trig likes milk-shakes and fizzy drinks.
Chip doesn't like milk-shakes or fizzy drinks.
Jenny likes pizza, but she doesn't like eggs.
Nick doesn't like eggs or pizza.
Trig likes eggs but he doesn't like pizza.
Chip doesn't like eggs or pizza.
Jenny likes steaks, but she doesn't like smelly bones.
Nick likes steaks, but he doesn't like smelly bones.
Trig doesn't like steaks or smelly bones.
Chip likes steaks and smelly bones.

5 Class game

Pupils' own answers. Follow example.

▶ PUPIL **A**   *I don't like snakes.*
   PUPIL **B**   *A doesn't like snakes and I don't like spinach.*
   PUPIL **C**   *A doesn't like snakes, B doesn't like spinach and I don't like horror films.*
   PUPIL **D**   *A doesn't like snakes . . .*

11 Do you like swimming?

Teaching aim

- Present simple in yes / no questions and short answers (see Chapters 9 and 10 for the affirmative form)

Vocabulary

chewing gum	hobby	popcorn	space films
finish	horror films	snails	spiders
glasses	ice-lollies		

Presentation

Ask pupils if they like swimming. Tell pupils that Jenny is answering questions about swimming here. Ask two pupils to read the text aloud like a dialogue. Ask pupils to pick out the questions.

Grammar lesson

Tell pupils to look at the tables in the grammar lesson to see how to make yes / no questions. Show that when **do** or **does** is used to make a question, the verb remains in the base form.

Explain how **do / does** is used in short answers then look at the examples.

Give pupils activity prompts (e.g. swimming, walking, eating) so that they ask questions with **like** and reply with short answers.

1 What do they do?

[oral / written   individual]

Aim: present simple in yes / no questions

Look at the examples with the pupils. Ask them why one sentence starts with **Do** and the other one with **Does**. Make sure that they understand why. Pupils read out the sentences adding either **Do** or **Does** at the beginning. Check their intonation. Pupils write in the answers. Make sure they don't forget the capital **D**.

Additional activity: Pupils say what they think are the correct short answers to the questions (they might have to use their imaginations a little).

2 A questionnaire

[oral / written   individual / partner]

Aim: present simple in yes / no questions (with **you** and **I**)

Discuss hobbies with the pupils and ask them to look at the different hobbies and interests listed in the exercise. Tell them to try and think of others. Based on the example shown, pupils write their own questionnaires using the hobbies listed and / or their own ideas. They then ask their partners the questions. The partners should give short answers.

Additional activity: Pupils report to the class on the results of their interviews.
  ▶ *John plays the piano.*

3 About you

[oral   partner / class]

Aim: present simple in short answers

Pupils read the questions and give true information about themselves in short answer form. This can be done round the class or with partners.

Additional activity: Each pupil writes one question like those in the exercise. He then asks five of his classmates who give short answers.

4 Do they like these things?

[oral   class]

Aim: present simple in yes / no questions and short answers (with **he** and **she**)

Tell pupils to look at the list of things Jenny and Nick **like** and **don't like**. Make sure they understand the vocabulary. They take turns asking and answering questions round the class as shown in the example.

Additional activity: In pairs, pupils make up their own list of likes and dislikes. They exchange it with another pair of pupils who ask and answer questions about it as before.

5 Class game: guessing jobs

[oral   class]

Aim: present simple in yes/no questions and short answers (with **you** and **I**)

Draw pupils' attention to the list of jobs and explain the meaning of any unknown vocabulary. Pupils look at the questions then write two or three of their own (they might need some help with this). Choose one pupil to mime a job from the list. The other pupils ask the questions from the list, or use the ones they have made up, to guess which job is being mimed. The pupil miming answers with 'Yes, I do', or 'No, I don't'. After the class has asked six questions, pupils take turns to guess the job. The pupil who guesses correctly then mimes a different job.

Additional activity: One pupil mimes and another one (who knows which job the first pupil is miming) answers the questions for him so that the questions must be asked and answered in the third person singular (**does** with **he** or **she**).

Answers

1 What do they do?

1	Do	9	Do
2	Do	10	Does
3	Does	11	Does
4	Does	12	Do
5	Does	13	Do
6	Do	14	Do
7	Do	15	Does
8	Does	16	Does

2 A questionnaire

Pupils' own answers.

3 About you

Pupils' own answers. Follow example.
► *Yes, I do.* OR *No, I don't.*

4 Do they like these things?

(Answers in any order.)

Does Jenny like pizza? Yes, she does.
Does Jenny like fizzy drinks? Yes, she does.
Does Jenny like chocolate? Yes, she does.
Does Jenny like sweets? Yes, she does.
Does Jenny like chewing gum? No, she doesn't.
Does Jenny like popcorn? No, she doesn't.
Does Jenny like crisps? No, she doesn't.
Does Jenny like peanuts? No, she doesn't.
Does Nick like popcorn? Yes, he does.
Does Nick like chewing gum? Yes, he does.
Does Nick like chocolate? Yes, he does.
Does Nick like Coke? Yes, he does.
Does Nick like pizza? No, he doesn't.
Does Nick like crisps? No, he doesn't.
Does Nick like sweets? No, he doesn't
Does Nick like ice-lollies? No, he doesn't.

5 Class game: guessing jobs

No fixed answers.

12 What do you do?

Student's book pages 30-33

Teaching aims

- Questions with **what**, **what time**, **when**, **where**, **who**, **why**, **how**, **how often** in the present simple (see Chapters 9, 10, 11 for other aspects of the present simple)
- Prepositions of time: **in**, **on**, **at**

Vocabulary

collect	outside	team
finish	summer	winter

Vocabulary

This presentation should be read as a dialogue from left to right. Ask one pupil to read Mr Bell's role and another one to read Tom's role. Make sure that pupils understand the questions. Ask them to find all the prepositions of time and time expressions. Write them on the board.

Grammar lesson

Explain the meaning of all the question words in the grammar lesson. Use the table to show how questions are formed. Tell pupils to substitute **he** with **you**, **I**, **we**, **they** and practise making other questions with regular verbs and **be**.

Look at the preposition section with pupils and explain how **in**, **on** and **at** are used with different time expressions. Point out the time expressions in the grammar lesson and ask pupils to think of others. Tell them that when something falls regularly on the same day of the week, we put an **s** at the end of the day (▶ *He goes to guitar lessons on Wednesdays.*). Ask pupils to make questions with **when** and **what time** and answer them with prepositions and time expressions.

1 What's wrong?

[written   individual]

Aim: word order in questions

Tell pupils that they must look at the boxes and put the words in the correct order to make questions. They write the sentences in the spaces provided.

Make sure that they remember to capitalize the first word and to include the question mark. Pupils can read out their answers.

Additional activity: Pupils write answers (true or fictive) to the questions.

2 Questions, questions, questions!

[oral / written   individual / partner]

Aim: question words and prepositions of time

Pupils take turns to read out the questions with **Where**, **When**, **What** or **How**. They then write in the answers.

Pupils ask their partners the questions. Their partners answer, giving true information about themselves, using prepositions of time where appropriate.

Additional activity: Each pupil writes his own answers to the questions.

3 Free time activities

[oral   individual / partner]

Aim: question words (**where**, **when**, **what**, **how**)

Pupils read the sentences then ask questions about them using the question words provided. Make sure that they understand that they are to ask for further information.

Additional activities:
- Pupils ask their partners the questions and the partners give true or fictive answers.
  - ▶ PUPIL 1   *I watch television.*
    PUPIL 2   *How often do you watch it?*
    PUPIL 1   *I watch it four times a week.*
- Pupils write out the questions and their partners' answers.
- Pupils write five new questions to ask their partners.

4 About Tom

[oral / written   individual / partner / class]

Aim: prepositions of time

a Pupils take turns to read the text aloud adding the correct preposition (**in**, **on**, or **at**). Then they write in the answers.

b Pupils read the questions and say the answers which they find in part **a**. This can be done as a class or with one partner asking the questions and the other one answering.

Additional activities:
- Pupils write out the answers to part **b**.
- Pupils transform the questions in part **b** in order to interview each other.
  - ▸ PUPIL 1   *What do you like best at school?*
    PUPIL 2   *I like . . .*

5 Favourite television programmes

[oral   individual / class]

Aim: prepositions of time

a Introduce the topic of television programmes. Look at the list of programmes with the pupils and make sure they understand the arrangement of the days of the week and the times. Review time telling if necessary. Pupils read the questions and look at the programme to find the answers. They answer, using prepositions of time as shown in the example.

b Each pupil asks three other pupils when their favourite television programmes are. The pupils answer, using prepositions of time as shown in the example.

Additional activity: Pupils say when their favourite television programme is on and the class must guess what it is.
  - ▸ PUPIL   *My favourite television programme is on Thursdays at eight o'clock.*
    CLASS   *Is it . . . ?*

Answers

1 What's wrong?

1 When do you play?
2 Where do you practise?
3 How often to you play?
4 When does the team practise?
5 Why do you like football?
6 When is the next game?
7 What time does it start?
8 When does it finish?
9 How often does Tom play?
10 Where does he play?

2 Questions, questions, questions!

1	When	9	When
2	What	10	What
3	When	11	When
4	How	12	What
5	When	13	What
6	Where	14	How
7	What	15	What
8	Where		

3 Free time activities

1 How often do you read them?
2 What (games) do you play?
3 Where do you go (at the weekend)?
4 What time do you swim (at the pool)?
5 What do you collect?
6 How often do you write to them?
7 Where do you play (football)?
8 What time do you take her (to school)?
9 When do you go (to the sports club)?
10 When do you watch them?
11 When do you take him (for a walk)?
12 How often do you go (to the youth club)?
13 What time do you go (to piano lessons)?
14 Where do you go (shopping)?

4 About Tom

a 1 On   6 in
   2 at   7 at
   3 on   8 in
   4 in   9 on
   5 In   10 at

b 1 Tom likes Games best.
   2 He has Games on Tuesdays and Fridays at two o'clock.
   3 He hates Maths because the teacher gives homework every day.
   4 He does his Maths homework on the bus on the way to school.
   5 School finishes at three thirty.
   6 He goes swimming on Saturday afternoons.
   7 He plays with his model railway in the evening.
   8 The school holidays are in summer and at Christmas and Easter.
   9 His birthday is in December, on the twenty-fifth.
  10 He gets a lot of presents at Christmas because it is his birthday.

5 Favourite television programmes

a 1 Sports World is on Saturdays at one thirty.
   2 Galaxies is on Mondays at seven o'clock.
   3 The Last Frontier is on Tuesdays and Thursdays at four thirty.
   4 Cartoon Time is on Mondays and Wednesdays at six o'clock.
   5 Friday Cinema is on Fridays at seven thirty.
   6 Space 4000 is on Saturdays at two thirty.
   7 Young Detectives is on Mondays at seven thirty.
   8 What's Next is on Wednesdays at four thirty.
   9 Video Club is on Tuesdays and Fridays at five o'clock.
  10 Seven Seas is on Wednesdays at seven o'clock.
  11 Questions and Answers is on Saturdays at one o'clock.
  12 Freddy is on Tuesdays and Thursdays at six thirty.
  13 The Martins is on Wednesdays at five thirty.
  14 Laserman is on Fridays at six o'clock.
  15 School's Out is on Fridays at six thirty.
  16 Walton Road is on Tuesdays at six o'clock.
  17 Junior Scientist is on Saturdays at twelve o'clock.
  18 Ghost Train is on Thursdays at six o'clock.

b Pupils' own answers. Follow example.

▶ PUPIL 1   *When is your favourite television programme?*
PUPIL 2   *It's on Wednesdays at seven o'clock.*

13 Slow down, Trig

Student's book pages 34–35

Teaching aim

- Imperatives

Vocabulary

cheat	litter	pick	touch
disturb	medicine	smoke	whistle
fire	park [vb]		

Presentation

Ask pupils to describe the pictures. Tell them that someone wants Trig to be careful. Read the text aloud as if talking to Trig.

Grammar lesson

Focus on the verbs in the presentation. Tell pupils that these are imperatives. Explain what imperatives are. Look at the different examples in the grammar lesson. Give other examples of orders, warnings, instructions and advice. Point out that exclamation marks are sometimes used with imperatives.

1 What do they say?

[oral   individual]

Aim: imperatives

Pupils read each sentence and decide whether it is their mother or their teacher who would say it. They transform the sentences as shown in the example. Remind pupils that sometimes the imperatives will be affirmative and sometimes they will be negative. Encourage them to use the right intonation.

Additional activity: Pupils write their answers in class or for homework.

2 Class instructions

[written / oral   individual]

Aim: imperatives

Tell pupils that they must talk like the teacher. Review the verbs in the list. Make sure pupils understand that sometimes they must use **Don't** before the verb. Pupils do the exercise orally, reading out the sentences. Then they write in the answers.

Additional activity: Each pupil writes down the three imperative sentences which he thinks the English teacher uses the most, then reads them out.

3 Signs

[oral   individual]

Aim: imperatives

Review the vocabulary in the lists. Ask pupils to look at the examples. They say what the different signs mean using the words from the list. Remind them that some of the signs tell them not to do something so they must say **Don't** before the verb.

Additional activity: Pupils draw signs which indicate rules for different places (their bedrooms, buses, swimming pools, classrooms etc.). The class must guess what the signs mean.

Answers

1 What do they say?

1 My mother says, 'Get up.'
2 My mother says, 'Don't eat chocolate before lunch.'
3 My mother says, 'Clean your teeth.'
4 My teacher says, 'Don't make a noise in class.'
5 My mother says, 'Wash your hands before meals.'
6 My mother says, 'Eat your vegetables.'
7 My mother says, 'Don't play loud music on the radio.'
8 My teacher says, 'Don't eat your lunch in class.'
9 My mother says, 'Help with the washing up.'
10 My mother says, 'Tidy your room.'
11 My teacher says, 'Don't read comics in class.'
12 My mother says, 'Don't jump on your bed.'
13 My teacher says, 'Do your English exercises.'
14 My mother says, 'Go to bed.'
15 My mother says, 'Don't play ball in the kitchen.'
16 My mother says, 'Make your bed.'
17 My teacher says, 'Don't fight in class.'
18 My teacher says, 'Don't sleep in class.'
19 My mother says, 'Feed the goldfish.'
20 My teacher says, 'Don't whistle in class.'
21 My teacher says, 'Don't write letters in class.'
22 My teacher says, 'Don't make paper aeroplanes in class.'
23 My mother says, 'Have a bath.'
24 My mother says, 'Don't hit your brother.'
25 My mother says, 'Don't watch television all day.'

2 Class instructions

1	Work	11	Play
2	Open	12	Find
3	Don't eat	13	Listen
4	Don't look	14	Sit
5	Work	15	Stand
6	Come / Go	16	Learn/Read/Write
7	Make / Write	17	Don't disturb
8	Don't look	18	Make
9	Answer	19	Speak
10	Write	20	Don't make

3 Signs

1 Don't overtake.
2 Don't touch.
3 Turn left.
4 Don't drink.
5 Don't smoke.
6 Don't park.
7 Don't pick flowers.
8 Go.
9 Don't talk.
10 Don't light fires.
11 Go straight on.
12 Don't play music.
13 Don't drop litter.
14 Don't take photographs.

14 What is there in Merton?

Student's book pages 36 – 39

Teaching aims

- **there is** and **there are**
  (see Chapter 5 for a review of the plural of nouns)
- Prepositions of place: **in**, **on**, **next to**, **between**, **behind**, **under**

Vocabulary

bank	library	post office	supermarket
bus stop	playground	suitcase	telephone box
hotel			

Presentation

Tell pupils that the picture is of the town of Merton where Jenny and Nick live. Ask pupils to look at the picture and identify the different shops and buildings in it. Read the text (or ask a pupil to read it) and ask pupils to point to the different things as they are mentioned. Use the picture to explain any prepositions of place the pupils don't understand.

Grammar lesson

Explain the difference between **there is** and **there are**. If necessary review plural and singular nouns. Point out that the short form **'s** is possible in the case of the singular form (**there's**). Explain how to make the negative, question and short answer forms. Ask pupils to look at the examples and make their own sentences with **there is** and **there are**.

Use the illustrations in the grammar lesson to explain the prepositions of place to the pupils. Ask questions about the position of different objects in the classroom so that pupils use prepositions of place to describe where they are.

1 Merton

[written   individual]

Aim: **there's**, **there isn't**, **there are**, **there aren't**, **is there** or **are there**

Pupils look at the map of Merton to fill in the spaces with the expressions provided. Tell them that sometimes the answers are negative and remind them to include capital letters for words beginning new sentences. Pupils can read out their answers.

Additional activity: In pairs, pupils take turns asking questions about Merton.
- ▶ *Is there a school in Park Street?*
  Yes, there is.

2 Littletown

[written   individual]

Aim: **there is**, **there are** and **next to**

Tell pupils that this is a street map of Littletown, a town near Merton. They look at the map and locate the places listed in the exercise. They write sentences using **There is** or **There are** and **next to** or the name of the street. Sometimes more than one answer is possible.

Additional activity: Pupils close their books and write as many sentences as they can about the buildings in Littletown with **There is / There are** and **next to** or the name of the street. The pupil with the most correct sentences wins.

3 Where you live

[oral   individual / partner]

Aim: **there is**, **there are**, **there isn't**, **there aren't**

Pupils must talk about the towns where they live. Make sure they understand the vocabulary. Pupils read the questions and give true short answers. They can either answer the questions individually or ask and answer the questions in pairs.

Additional activity: Pupils write sentences about their towns using the prompts from Exercise 2 and **There is / There are**.
- ▶ School
  There is a school next to . . .

4 Where are Nick's things?

[written   individual]

Aim: prepositions of place – **in**, **on**, **next to**, **between**, **behind**, **under**

Tell pupils to look at the picture of Nick's untidy room. Make sure that they understand all the vocabulary on the right (both nouns and prepositions). They write sentences to describe where the things are in Nick's room. Sometimes there are several ways of saying where the things are.

Additional activity: In pairs, pupils ask questions about the objects in the picture.
▶ PUPIL 1   *Is the guitar on the chair?*
   PUPIL 2   *Yes, it is.*

5 Memory game

[oral   class]

Aim: prepositions of place – **in**, **on**, **next to**, **between**, **behind**, **under**

Pupils look at the picture of Nick's messy room again for one minutes (or less). Then they cover the page and say the answers to the questions using prepositions of place. Make sure they get the pronouns right (**it** or **they**).

Additional activity: Pupils do the same as above but write down the answers and see how many they get right.

Answers

1 Merton

1	there's	8	there isn't
2	there's	9	Is there
3	There are	10	there isn't
4	There's	11	there's
5	there's	12	are there
6	There are	13	are there
7	there aren't	14	Is there

2 Littletown

1 There is a hotel next to the car park (OR in Elm Street).
2 There is a restaurant in King Street (OR next to the car park).
3 There are car parks next to the hotel and next to the restaurant.
4 There is a supermarket in South street (OR next to the post office).
5 There is a sports centre in South Street (OR next to the bank).
6 There is a post office next to the supermarket.
7 There are bus stops in South Street and in North Street.
8 There is a garage in South Street (OR next to the supermarket).
9 There are shops in King Street.
10 There are cafés in Wood Street and in North Street.
11 There is a library in North Street (OR next to the bank).
12 There are banks next to the library and next to the sports centre (OR in South Street).

3 Where you live

Pupils' own answers.

▶ *Yes, there is / are.* OR *No, there isn't / aren't.*

4 Where are Nick's things?

1   His books are on the chair (and on the floor).
2   His guitar is on the floor (between the bed and the cupboard)
3   His skateboard is in the basket.
4   His keys are on the floor (next to the chair).
5   His alarm clock is under the bed (on the floor).
6   His tennis racket is on the chair.
7   His shoes are on the bed.
8   His suitcase is behind the guitar (between the bed and the cupboard).
9   His school bag is on the floor.
10 His cap and scarf are on the doorknob.
11 His jacket is in the cupboard.
12 His radio is on the desk.

5 Memory game

1   It's on the floor.
2   It's on the chair.
3   They're on the floor, under the desk.
4   It's on the desk.
5   They're on the doorknob.
6   It's in the cupboard.
7   They're on the chair (and on the floor).
8   It's in the basket.
9   It's on the floor (between the bed and the cupboard).
10 They're on the floor, next to the chair.

15 Can he speak English?

Teaching aim

- **can** for ability
  (see Chapter 18 for **can** for permission)

Vocabulary

bear	lion	sheep	spider
climb	ride	speak	toad

Presentation

Explain that Trig is listening at the door to people talking about him in another room. They are talking about what he can and cannot do. Read the presentation to the pupils. Ask pupils what they think **can** means.

Grammar lesson

Ask pupils to look at the verb tables. Point out that **can** and **cannot** are the same with all pronouns. Tell pupils they can use **cannot** or **can't** for the negative form. Pupils practise the form by adding *speak English* or other activities (*sing, sew, cook* etc.). Choose pupils to read the question and short answer forms.

1 Things you can do

[oral   individual]

Aim: **can** for ability

Tell pupils to look at each group of pictures and explain that the word in the middle goes with the activities surrounding it. Review the vocabulary with them. Pupils make sentences about what they can and cannot do, as shown in the example.

Additional activities:
- Pupils write the sentences from the exercise in class or for homework.
- Pupils choose one of the verbs from the exercise and draw their own illustrations around it. They exchange it with their partners who must say what they **can** and **cannot** (or **can't**) do.

2 Can elephants fly?

[written   individual]

Aim: **can** for ability

Some of the facts are right and some are wrong. Tell pupils to read the sentences. Make sure they understand them. Pupils write **Right** or **Wrong** followed by the correct sentence.

Additional activity: Each pupil writes five sentences like the ones in the exercise – some right and some wrong. Their partners read the sentences and say if they are right or wrong in the same way as in the exercise.

3 What can they do?

[oral   individual / class]

Aim: **can** for ability

a   Tell pupils that the table shows which activities the characters can and cannot do. Review the vocabulary with them. Explain that a ✔ means that a character can do something and a ✗ means that a character can't do it. Pupils make sentences, as shown in the example. Remind them that it is possible to use either **can't** or **cannot** in the negative form.

b   Pupils use the activities from the table as prompts to take turns asking and answering questions as shown in the example.

Additional activity: Using the list of activities, pupils write sentences about what they (*I . . .*) and their partners (*He / She . . .*) can and can't do.
  ► *I can swim under water.*

Answers

1 Things you can do

Pupils' own answers. Follow examples.

► *I can speak English but I can't speak French.*
► *I can play football and I can play table tennis.*

The activities are:

speak English, German, French, Greek
play the piano, the trumpet, the violin,
   the guitar
use a calculator, a computer, a camera,
   a typewriter
play football, table tennis (or ping pong),
   basketball, tennis
ride a horse, a bicycle (or a bike), a camel,
   a motorcycle

2 Can elephants fly?

1 Right. Penguins can swim.
2 Wrong. Penguins can't fly.
3 Right. Horses can swim.
4 Right. Lions can climb trees.
5 Wrong. Elephants can't catch fish.
6 Wrong. Dogs can't climb trees.
7 Right. Parrots can fly.
8 Wrong. Cats can't fly.
9 Right. Camels can run.
10 Right. Bears can catch fish.
11 Wrong. Spiders can't swim.
12 Right. Sheep can jump.

3 What can they do?

a 1 Jenny, Nick and Amanda can dive.
   Tom can't.
2 Nick and Amanda can put up a tent.
   Jenny and Tom can't.
3 Nick, Amanda and Tom can row a boat.
   Jenny can't.
4 Nick and Amanda can make a camp fire.
   Jenny and Tom can't.
5 Jenny and Amanda can sew on a button.
   Nick and Tom can't.
6 Jenny and Tom can make an omelette.
   Nick and Amanda can't.
7 Nick, Tom and Amanda can tie knots.
   Jenny can't.
8 Jenny, Nick and Amanda can do first aid.
   Tom can't.
9 Nick, Tom and Amanda can climb a rope.
   Jenny can't.
10 Jenny, Tom and Amanda can read a map.
   Nick can't.

b Pupils' own answers. Follow example.
   ► PUPIL 1 *Can you swim under water?*
      PUPIL 2 *Yes, I can.* OR *No, I can't.*

16 Trig is helping

Student's book pages 42 – 45

Teaching aim

- Present continuous: **be** + **ing** form
  (see Chapter 1 for a review of **be**)

Vocabulary

catch	dish	help	kick
clap	drop	jump	whistle
dig	hang		

Presentation

Ask pupils to look at the pictures in the presentation. Tell pupils that these actions are happening now. Read the text. Ask pupils to find the verbs. Write them on the board.

Grammar lesson

Explain that the present continuous is used to talk about what is happening now and for that reason is often used with words such as **now**, **at the moment**, **today**. Use the information in the grammar lesson to show pupils how the **ing** form of verbs is made (you might need to review consonants and vowels with them) and then how the present continuous is made. Tell pupils to read the examples in the grammar lesson. Ask them to practise saying both long and short forms with different pronouns and verbs. Correct their pronunciation.

Ask pupils to look at the presentation section pictures again. They must cover the text and use verbs in the present continuous to say what is happening.

1 What is he writing?

[written individual]

Aim: the **ing** form of verbs

Tell pupils that Trig needs help writing the **ing** form of verbs. If necessary, remind them how to make the **ing** form. Pupils read the verbs then write in the correct **ing** forms in the spaces provided. They can read out their answers. Correct their pronunciation.

Additional activities:
- Tell pupils to cover the grammar lesson. Prompt them with a pronoun and a verb (base form). Pupils must transform them into the present continuous form.
  - ▶ Y O U   *he wash*
    P U P I L   *He is washing.*
- Do the same as above but with the question, negative and short answer forms.

2 At home with the Bells

[oral / written individual]

Aim: present continuous

Pupils read through the text saying the correct verb in the present continuous tense. They write in the answers. If pupils have trouble finding the correct verbs, tell them to read the presentation again.

Additional activity: In pairs, pupils ask questions about the text and reply with short answers.
- ▶ P U P I L 1   *Is the sun shining?*
    P U P I L 2   *Yes, it is.*

3 What are they doing now?

[oral / written   individual]

Aim: present continuous

a Tell pupils that they must imagine that it is now Sunday afternoon and the Allens are visiting the Bells in their garden. Pupils read the text and look at the picture in order to say what the characters are doing. They use the verbs from the list and say them in the present continuous form. Then they write the answers in class or for homework.

b Pupils look at the picture again to say the answers to the questions as in the example (negative short answer, then affirmative answer).

Additional activity: Each pupil writes a question like the ones in **b** and reads it to the class. The class answers it.

4 Trig's first football match

[oral   individual]

Aim: questions with **why** in the present continuous

Remind pupils that Trig is from another planet and doesn't understand things like football. Review the vocabulary in the box. Pupils look at the pictures and say the questions that Trig would ask using words from each box.

Additional activities:
● Pupils write the questions in class or for homework.
● Pupils write affirmative sentences about what the people in the pictures are doing.

5 Miming game

[oral   class]

Aim: questions and short answers in the present continuous

One pupil mimes an action. The other pupils in the class ask questions to find out what he is doing. The pupil who guesses correctly then mimes a different action.

Additional activity: Divide the class into two teams. Choose an action and whisper it to one pupil from each team who mime it for their teams. The teams ask questions in the present continuous to guess the action as quickly as possible. The first team to guess it gets a point. The first team to get 10 (or 5) points wins.

Answers

1 What is he writing?

1	having	16	learning
2	swimming	17	catching
3	taking	18	sitting
4	stopping	19	raining
5	flying	20	hitting
6	speaking	21	looking
7	using	22	going
8	making	23	dropping
9	eating	24	chasing
10	helping	25	walking
11	putting	26	baking
12	reading	27	kicking
13	getting	28	clapping
14	watching	29	carrying
15	coming	30	giving

2 At home with the Bells

1	shining	6	running
2	hanging	7	doing
3	washing	8	helping
4	digging	9	hanging
5	doing		

3 What are they doing now?

a
1	is sitting	7	is running
2	is talking	8	is hiding
3	are drinking	9	is talking
4	is playing	10	are standing
5	is eating	11	are looking
6	is having	12	is sleeping

b
1 No, they aren't. They're sitting.
2 No, he isn't. He's running.
3 No, they aren't. They're playing ball.
4 No, it isn't. It's hiding.
5 No he isn't. He's sleeping.
6 No, they aren't. They're talking.
7 No, he isn't. He's eating.

4   Trig's first football match

1   Why are they running?
2   Why is he kicking the ball?
3   Why is she jumping up and down?
4   Why are they shouting?
5   Why are they sleeping?
6   Why are they carrying a player?
7   Why is he hitting the ball with his head?
8   Why are they singing?
9   Why is he blowing the whistle?
10   Why are they clapping?

5   Miming game

No fixed answers. Follow example.

▶   CLASS   *Are you cleaning something?*
    PUPIL   *No, I'm not.*
    CLASS   *Are you playing a game?*
    PUPIL   *No, I'm not.*
    CLASS   *Are you opening a window?*
    PUPIL   *Yes, I am.*

17 Can you see them?

Student's book pages 46–49

Teaching aims

- Object pronouns – **me**, **you**, **him**, **her**, **it**, **us**, **you**, **them**
- **like**, **love**, **hate** + **ing** form

Vocabulary

camping	free time	museum	science fiction
chase	hide	opera	travelling

Presentation

Tell pupils to look at the picture. Ask them what Jenny and Nick are doing. Ask them what Trig is doing. Ask three pupils to read the speech bubbles of the different characters. Make sure pupils understand the text.

Grammar lesson

Review subject pronouns and their function in a sentence. Introduce object pronouns. Tell pupils to look at the table and practise saying the object pronouns. Explain that they follow verbs and prepositions (review prepositions if necessary). Draw attention to the examples. Ask pupils to find the object pronouns in the presentation section and read out the sentences. Ask them to make other sentences with different object pronouns.

Introduce the structure **like**, **love**, **hate** + **ing**. Explain the meaning of **like**, **love** and **hate**, and how they are used with other verbs +**ing**. Point out that this structure is not the same as the present continuous tense. Ask the pupils to talk about what they like, love or hate doing.

Read the presentation section again.

1 Missing things

[oral / written   individual]

Aim: object pronouns – **me**, **you**, **him**, **her**, **it**, **us**, **them**

Tell pupils that Nick and Jenny are looking for their things but they can't find them. Ask pupils to take turns reading Jenny and Nick's roles aloud. They must add the correct object pronouns. Then they write the answers in class or for homework.

Additional activity: Ask pupils to look at the sentences again and say which words the object pronouns replace.

► them
  my coloured pencils

2 Jenny's list

[oral   individual]

Aim: object pronouns – **him**, **her**, **it**, **them**

Tell pupils that Jenny has made a list of the things and people she likes and doesn't like at school. Pupils take turns reading the questions and answering them with information from the list. Remind them that they must replace the things and people with object pronouns.

Additional activity: Pupils write the answers to the questions in class or for homework.

3 Sports

[oral / written   individual / partner]

Aim: object pronouns – **her**, **him**, **it**, **them**

a Talk to pupils about games and sports and ask them which ones they like, etc. Explain that Nick has written his sports favourites on the questionnaire and that when Tom agrees with Nick he has written a ✓ but when he disagrees, he has written a ✕. Pupils look at the examples and then say similar sentences about Nick and Tom's favourites using object pronouns. (Remind pupils what **too** means if they cannot remember.)

sports team is treated as a plural here but it is equally correct to treat it as a singular.

b Pupils fill in the blank questionnaire themselves by writing in their own sports favourites. They exchange lists with their partners. Pupils read the lists and, if they like them too, put a ✓, or if they don't like them, put a ✕. They write sentences using object pronouns, based on the examples. They can read their sentences out to the class.

Additional activity: Pupils write new lists and repeat part **b** with different partners. This can be done several times.

4 In your free time

[written   individual]

Aim: **like**, **love**, **hate** + **ing**

Ask pupils what they love doing, what they like doing and what they hate doing. Review the use of **like**, **love**, **hate** + **ing** if necessary. Make sure pupils understand the vocabulary in the exercise. They read the prompts then write sentences stating whether they like, love or hate doing the different activities.

Additional activity: Pupils exchange books with a partner. The partner reads the sentences and puts a ✓ beside those sentences he agrees with and a ✕ beside those sentences he disagrees with. He returns the book to the first pupil who makes sentences like those in Exercise 3.

▶ *I love drawing and . . . loves it too.* O R *I love drawing but . . . doesn't love it.*

5 What do you like?

[oral   partner]

Aim: **like**, **love**, **hate** + **ing**

Review the vocabulary with the pupils. In pairs, pupils read the prompts and make questions with them and **like** + **ing** as shown in the example. Their partners must give true answers to the questions using **love** or **hate** + **ing**.

Additional activities:
- Pupils write their answers in class or for homework.
- Pupils look at the activities in Exercises 4 and 5 and write five sentences about the ones they hate doing the most and five sentences about the ones they love doing the most. They read their sentences out to the class.
  ▶ *I love singing.*

Answers

1 Missing things

1	it	8	it
2	me	9	me
3	her	10	you
4	it	11	her
5	me	12	us
6	you	13	him
7	them	14	them

2 Jenny's list

1   Yes, she likes her.
2   No, she doesn't like him.
3   No, she doesn't like them.
4   Yes, she likes her.
5   No, she doesn't like it.
6   No, she doesn't like them.
7   Yes, she likes them.
8   No, she doesn't like him.
9   No, she doesn't like her.
10 Yes, she likes him.
11 Yes, she likes it.
12 Yes, she likes it.

Yes, I like it. OR No, I don't like it.

3 Sports

a Nick likes Manchester United but Tom doesn't like them.

Nick likes football and Tom likes it too.

Nick likes golf but Tom doesn't like it.

Nick likes Ferraris and Tom likes them too.

b Pupils' own answers. Follow examples.
  ▶ *I like Steffi Graf and Tom likes her too.*
  ▶ *I like Carl Lewis but Tom doesn't like him.*

4 In your free time

Pupils' own answers. Follow example.
  ▶ *I like drawing.*

5 What do you like?

Pupils' own answers. Follow example.
  ▶ playing tennis
    PUPIL 1   *Do you like playing tennis?*
    PUPIL 2   *Yes, I love playing tennis.* OR
          No, I hate playing tennis.

18 I can, but you mustn't

Student's book pages 50 – 51

Teaching aims

- **can** for permission
  (see Chapter 15 for **can** for ability)
- **must** for necessity

Vocabulary

borrow	felt pen	scissors	toothpaste
cold [n]	horror film	squirt	water pistol
dirty	noise		

Presentation

Ask pupils about the meaning of **can** which they have already learned (for ability). Ask them to give you some examples of sentences with it. Tell them they are going to learn a new meaning for it. Read through the presentation with them and ask them what they think it means.

Grammar lesson

Tell pupils to look at the examples in the grammar box. Explain how in all these cases **can** is used to ask for permission. Ask pupils to give new examples of sentences with **can**. Write them on the board. Remind pupils that **can** has two negative forms: **cannot** and **can't**.

Read through the presentation again to reinforce the use of **can** and draw the pupils' attention to **must**. Ask them what they think it means. Explain it.

Pupils practise saying the **must** form in the grammar lesson. Correct their pronunciation – tell them not to pronounce the first **t** in **mustn't**. Explain that there is no **s** for verbs with **he / she / it** and that **to** never follows **must**. Read the examples and ask them to make other sentences about things you must and must not do.

1 Can you or can't you?

[oral   class]

Aim: **can** for permission

One pupil asks questions with **Can I . . .?** and another pupil plays his father, mother, doctor etc. and gives a short answer. This exercise can be done several times. Pupils should take turns asking and answering.

Additional activity: Pupils write questions with **Can I . . .?** which they would normally ask one particular person (mother, father, teacher etc.). They read the questions to the class and the class says who they would address the question to.

> PUPIL   *Can I have some bread?*
> CLASS   *You ask the baker.*

2 Ask your partner

[oral   partner]

Aim: **can** for permission

Ask pupils if they borrow other people's things (explain what **borrow** means). Make sure pupils know all the vocabulary. Pupils ask their partners if they can borrow the objects by making questions with **can**. The answers can be in the affirmative or negative form.

Additional activities:
- Pupils repeat the answers but replace **can't** with **cannot**.
- Pupils follow the model but talk about other objects that they have in their desks or school bags.
- Pupils write questions and answers in class or for homework.

3 Classroom rules

[oral / written   individual]

Aim: **must** for necessity

Talk about rules in the classroom and what pupils must and mustn't do. Pupils read out the sentences completing them with **must** or **mustn't** (their answers might provoke some discussion). Pupils write the answers in class or for homework.

Additional activity: In pairs, pupils write a list of ten of their own rules with **must** for their ideal classroom.

4 Necessity

[oral/written   individual]

Aim: **must** for necessity

Make sure pupils understand the vocabulary and context of each sentence. They read the sentences and say what the characters must or mustn't do. Pupils write the answers in class or for homework.

Additional activity: Each pupil chooses a sentence from the exercise and draws a picture to illustrate it. He shows the picture to the class and they must say the correct sentence.

Answers

1 Can you or can't you?

All questions begin with **Can I**, as in the example.

▶ *Can I go to see a horror film?*

Probable answers to the questions:

1	No, you can't.	6	No, you can't.
2	No, you can't.	7	Yes, you can.
3	Yes, you can.	8	No, you can't.
4	No, you can't.	9	No, you can't.
5	Yes, you can.	10	Yes, you can.

2 Ask your partner

The answer to all the questions is:
Yes, you can. OR *No, you can't.*

1 Can I borrow your ruler, please?
2 Can I borrow your pen, please?
3 Can I borrow your rubber, please?
4 Can I borrow your pencil sharpener, please?
5 Can I borrow your scissors, please?
6 Can I borrow your grammar book, please?
7 Can I borrow your dictionary, please?
8 Can I borrow your felt pen, please?
9 Can I borrow your coursebook, please?
10 Can I borrow your sticky tape, please?
11 Can I borrow your atlas, please?
12 Can I borrow your glue, please?

3 Classroom rules

Probable answers:

1	We mustn't	9	We must
2	We must	10	We must
3	We mustn't	11	We mustn't
4	We must	12	We mustn't
5	We mustn't	13	We must
6	We must	14	We mustn't
7	We mustn't	15	We mustn't
8	We mustn't	16	We mustn't

4 Necessity

1	mustn't	9	must
2	must	10	mustn't
3	mustn't	11	mustn't
4	must	12	must
5	mustn't	13	mustn't
6	mustn't	14	must
7	mustn't	15	must
8	mustn't		

19 How much milk?

Student's book pages 52 – 55

Teaching aims

- **some** and **any** with countable and uncountable nouns
- **how much** and **how many** with countable and uncountable nouns
  (see Chapter 8 for countable and uncountable nouns)

Vocabulary

cocoa	fridge	margarine	rain
dates	jam	potato	toffee
flour	lemon cake		

Presentation

Ask pupils if they like to cook and what they like to cook. Ask them to name different ingredients used for cooking. Make a list on the board.

Tell pupils that Nick and Jenny are making a cake. Read the text. Use the picture to help explain any vocabulary pupils don't understand.

Grammar lesson

Review countable and uncountable nouns. Divide the words already written on the board into lists of countable and uncountable nouns. Ask pupils to put the nouns from the text into the countable or uncountable list.

Explain the different uses of **some** and **any** listed in the grammar lesson. Read the examples with the pupils. Ask them to give other examples with the words on the board.

Ask pupils to look at the presentation section again and find **how much** and **how many**. Ask why these are different. Refer to the examples in the grammar lesson. Tell pupils to make questions with **how much** or **how many** and the words on the board.

1 Making a cake

[oral / written   individual]

Aim: **some** and **any** with countable and uncountable nouns

Ask pupils what is needed to make a chocolate cake. Write down some of the vocabulary to make sure they are familiar with it. Pupils take turns reading the text and putting **some** or **any** in the gaps. Then they write in the answers.

Additional activity: In pairs, pupils make a list of the ingredients for the chocolate cake and take turns asking each other if Nick and Jenny have got any.
- ▶ *Have they got any margarine?*
  No, they haven't got any.

2 Memory game

[oral   partner / class]

Aim: **a / an** or **some** with countable and uncountable nouns

Pupils must look at the picture for one minute. Then they close their books and say what's on the table, using **a / an** or **some**. This can be done as a class or in pairs with one partner trying to name what's on the table and the other one looking at the picture to check the answers.

Additional activity: Pupils close their books and write down what's on the table with **a / an** or **some**.

3 Is there any?

[oral   partner]

Aim: **some** and **any** with countable and uncountable nouns

In pairs, pupils look at the picture in Exercise 2 again. One partner asks questions about what is on the table and the other one gives correct answers. Tell the pupils who are asking the questions to use the right form of the verb **be** (*Is there . . .* or *Are there . . .*). Remind pupils that we use **some** in positive sentences and **any** in negative sentences.

Additional activity: Pupils do the same thing again but the one who is answering the questions must have his or her book closed and answer from memory.

4 More cooking

[written   individual]

Aim: **some** and **any** with countable and uncountable nouns

Pupils look at the prepared food and drink items on the left and then look at the ingredients to their right. They must use **some** and **any** to write sentences about what is needed and what isn't needed to make the things.

Additional activity: Pupils make their own 'funny recipes' like the ones in this exercise. Their partners use **some** and **any** to say what is needed and what isn't needed to make them. It might be helpful to write some countable and uncountable vocabulary on the board before starting.

5 Interview

[oral   partner]

Aim: **how much** and **how many**

Pupils make questions by adding **How much** or **How many** to the beginning of each sentence. Their partners give true answers to the questions.

Additional activities:
- Pupils write the questions in class or for homework.
- Each pupil writes a new question with **How much** or **How many** and puts it to five of his classmates.

6 Puzzle

[written   individual]

Aim: **some**, **any**; **how much**, **how many**; countable and uncountable nouns

Pupils read the sentences and write in the correct words. Then they complete the puzzle.

Additional activity: Pupils read out the correctly completed sentences.

Answers

1 Making a cake

1	any	6	some
2	any	7	any
3	some	8	some
4	some	9	any
5	some	10	any

2 Memory game

(Answers in any order)

some meat	a banana
some bread	a pear
some rice	a pineapple
some coffee	an onion
some tea	an egg
some orange juice	
some apples	
some cherries	
some grapes	

3 Is there any?

1. Is there any coffee?
   Yes, there's some coffee.
2. Is there any bread?
   Yes, there's some bread.
3. Is there any cheese?
   No, there isn't any cheese.
4. Are there any apples?
   Yes, there are some apples.
5. Is there any orange juice?
   Yes, there's some orange juice.
6. Are there any potatoes?
   No, there aren't any potatoes.
7. Is there any milk?
   No, there isn't any milk.
8. Is there any meat?
   Yes, there's some meat.
9. Are there any tomatoes?
   No, there aren't any tomatoes.
10. Is there any tea?
    Yes, there's some tea.
11. Is there any flour?
    No, there isn't any flour.
12. Is there any chocolate?
    No, there isn't any chocolate.
13. Are there any cherries?
    Yes, there are some cherries.
14. Is there any sugar?
    No, there isn't any sugar.
15. Are there any grapes?
    Yes, there are some grapes.
16. Are there any dates?
    No, there aren't any dates.

4 More cooking

1. I need some strawberries and some sugar. I don't need any carrots or any olives.
2. I need some eggs, some milk and some cheese. I don't need any bananas, any chocolate or any grapes.
3. I need some flour, some butter, some lemons and some sugar. I don't need any fish or any onions.
4. I need some water, some tea, some sugar and some milk. I don't need any cherries or any eggs.
5. I need some bananas, some milk and some ice cream. I don't need any tomatoes or any pepper.

5 Interview

1	How much	6	How much
2	How many	7	How many
3	How much	8	How many
4	How many	9	How many
5	How much	10	How much

6 Puzzle

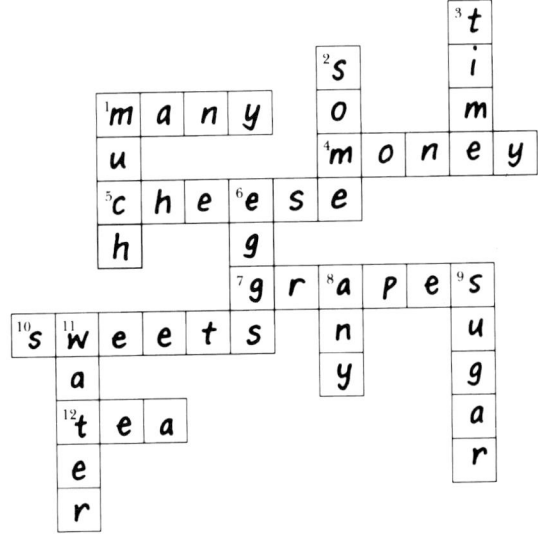

Across

4 money
5 cheese
7 grapes
10 sweets
12 tea

Down

1 much
2 some
3 time
6 eggs
8 any
9 sugar
11 water

20 How often do you help?

Student's book pages 56 – 59

Teaching aim

- Adverbs of frequency: **never**, **rarely**, **sometimes** etc.

Vocabulary

abroad	chewing gum	present
break	haircut	tidy
busy	mess	traffic

Presentation

Before they read the text, ask pupils how often they think Nick helps in the house. Tell them that the picture is of Nick's room. Ask them to read the text. Make sure they understand it.

Grammar lesson

Introduce adverbs of frequency. Explain what an adverb is. Ask pupils to pick out the verbs in the text and then the adverbs.

Ask pupils to look at the graph which shows the relationship between **never**, **rarely**, **sometimes**, **usually**, **always** and **often**. Ask them how often they help in the house. Tell them to answer with one of these adverbs of frequency.

Point out the position of adverbs of frequency in a sentence with **be** and with other verbs. Pupils practise making sentences of both types.

Explain that there are other ways of expressing frequency. Tell pupils to look at the list in the grammar box but explain that you can make many more with different expressions of time. You might use a calendar to illustrate the examples. Try making as many expressions of frequency as you can with the pupils' help. Write several sentences on the board showing where the time expressions are positioned.

1 Tell the truth!

[oral / written   individual]

Aim: adverbs of frequency – **never**, **rarely**, **sometimes**, **usually**, **often**, **always**

Pupils use adverbs of frequency to make true sentences about themselves. Make sure they understand the vocabulary. Pupils write in their answers then they read out the sentences to the class. You might query some of their responses (just as Jenny queries Trig's in the example).

Additional activity: Pupils write one sentence for each adverb of frequency and read the sentences to the class.

2 Tell the truth – again!

[written   individual]

Aim: adverbs of frequency – **never**, **rarely**, **sometimes**, **usually**, **often**, **always**

Pupils make sentences giving true information about themselves, as Trig does in the example. Read through the exercise with them, making sure they understand all the sentences. Then let them write in their answers. Pupils can take turns reading each answer to the class.

Additional activity: Pupils think up sentences like those in the exercise. Write some of them on the board. Ask pupils to use these sentences to make new ones about themselves with adverbs of frequency.

3 Holidays

[written   individual]

Aim: adverbs of frequency (position)

Talk about holidays, where the pupils and their families go etc. Then talk about the Bells' holidays and what they usually do. Read through the sentences to make sure pupils understand them. Pupils rewrite the sentences inserting the adverb of frequency indicated in brackets in the correct position.

Additional activity: In pairs, one pupil closes his book and the other pupil asks him yes / no questions about the Bells' holidays. The pupil asking questions should ask several questions with the answer 'No'.

▶ PUPIL 1   *Do the Bells always take the car abroad?*
   PUPIL 2   *No, they never do.*

4 How often do you . . .?

[written   individual]

Aim: expressions of frequency

Draw attention to the different possible expressions of frequency and practise saying them with the pupils (**once a day**, **twice a day**, **three times a day** etc.). Read over the questions to make sure pupils understand the vocabulary. Pupils write true answers to the questions. They can take turns reading them out to the class.

Additional activity: Each pupil makes up two questions with **how often** and asks other pupils in the class. He must keep track of the answers and report them to the class.

▶ *Five pupils go to the doctor's once a year, three pupils go to the doctor's twice a year etc.*

5 Class game

[oral / written   class]

Aim: expressions of frequency

Each pupil takes a piece of paper and writes an action with **I . . .** on the left hand half of it. He folds the paper over so that what has been written is at the back. His partner then writes an expression of frequency on the other side of the fold. Tell pupils that they can use any expressions of frequency they can think up. One of the partners unfolds the paper and reads the sentence to the class.

Additional activity: Pupils change partners and do the same exercise over again. You can repeat this as many times as you like.

Answers

1 **Tell the truth!**

Pupils' own answers. Follow example.
▶ I *never* do bad things!

2 **Tell the truth – again!**

Pupils' own answers. The adverb goes before the verb in every sentence. Follow example.
▶ I eat sweets.
I never eat sweets.

3 **Holidays**

1 They rarely stay in England.
2 They sometimes drive to Scotland or Wales.
3 In August there is often a lot of traffic on the roads.
4 They sometimes go to Greece or Spain.
5 In August the weather is usually wonderful there.
6 They never take the car abroad.
7 Before the holidays Nick and Jenny are always excited.
8 Chip always goes with them to Scotland or Wales.
9 When they go abroad, he usually stays with the Allens or with the Todds.
10 But unfortunately he isn't always a good dog.

4 **How often do you . . .?**

Pupils' own answers. **once a day** or **every morning** etc. goes at the end of every sentence.
▶ How often do you wash your face?
I wash my face three times a day.

5 **Class game**

Pupils' own answers. Follow examples.
▶ *I clean my shoes once a year.*
I clean my shoes ten times a day.

21 Tom plays football

Student's book pages 60–63

Teaching aims

- Comparison of the present simple and present continuous
  (see Chapters 9–11 for the present simple and Chapter 16 for the present continuous)
- **let's**

Vocabulary

chase	fall [vb]	mow
chess	ironing	nurse
dancer	light [n]	reporter

Presentation

Ask pupils to say what they know about Nick and Tom. On the board, write a few sentences about each character in the present simple tense.

Read the text aloud with the pupils.

Grammar lesson

Ask pupils to identify the tense of the sentences on the board. Ask them to help you review the present simple tense.

Ask pupils to find sentences in the presentation which are not in the present simple tense. Pupils must then help you review the present continuous tense.

Compare the two tenses by looking at the examples in the grammar lesson with the pupils. Ask pupils to give other examples.

Remind them that the present continuous is often accompanied by words like **now**, **just now**, **at the moment** etc.

Introduce **let's**. Tell pupils to read the example sentences in the grammar lesson. Ask them to give you other examples of sentences with **let's**. Explain that the negative form of **let's** is **let's not**.

1 What are they?
What are they doing?

[oral / written   individual]

Aim: comparison of the present simple and present continuous

Tell pupils to look at the two questions in the heading and say which tenses they are in. Ask them which tense they expect the answers to be in.

Make sure pupils understand the vocabulary in the list of occupations. Ask them to look at the example picture and sentences. Make sure pupils understand which tenses they have been written in and why.

Pupils write two sentences below each picture. Then they read them out to the class.

Additional activity: Pupils take turns asking and answering questions about the pictures without reading what they have written (this can also be done before pupils write in the answers).

▶ PUPIL 1   *What is she doing?*
   PUPIL 2   *She is eating.*
   PUPIL 1   *What is she?*
   PUPIL 2   *She is a nurse.*

2 It's the wrong day

[written   individual]

Aim: comparison of the present simple and present continuous

Tell pupils that the two lists are Mr and Mrs Bell's usual weekly programmes. Today is Tuesday but they are doing things they usually do on other days.

Pupils look at the pictures and write sentences about what the Bells are doing and what they usually do.

Additional activity: In pairs, one pupil reads out his sentences and his partner identifies which picture he is talking about (without reading his own answers).

▶ PUPIL 1   *She is doing the shopping today.*
         She usually does the shopping on Mondays.
   PUPIL 2   *Picture 5.*

3 Zoe and Anna

[oral   partner]

Aim: comparison of present simple and present continuous

a Tell pupils they are going to talk about Zoe. Remind them how to ask questions with the present simple and the present continuous.

Both partners look at the picture of Zoe. One partner reads the text aloud or they both read silently. The first partner then asks questions about Zoe in the present simple and in the present continuous. The second partner must answer the questions in the correct tense.

b Tell the pupils they are going to talk about Anna who is very different from Zoe. Follow the same instructions as for **a** but the partners must switch roles.

Additional activity: Each pupil writes five sentences about Zoe and Anna.
► *Zoe likes speaking English but Anna doesn't.*
► *Zoe is laughing but Anna isn't.*

4 Let's . . .

[oral / written   individual]

Aim: **let's**

Tell pupils that they must make suggestions with **let's**. Read through the list of possible suggestions to make sure they understand the vocabulary. Pupils take turns to say correct sentences with **let's** and the words from the list. They write the answers in class or for homework.

Additional activity: Each pupil chooses one of the sentences and draws a picture to illustrate it. The other pupils in the class must say the sentence that goes with it, with **let's**.

Answers

---

1 What are they? What are they doing?

1 He is a doctor. He is dancing.
2 They are dancers. They are falling.
3 They are boys. They are sleeping.
4 He is a farmer. He is drinking.
5 He is a policeman. He is singing.
6 She is a reporter. She is running.
7 They are pilots. They are playing football.
8 They are astronauts. They are playing golf.

---

2 It's the wrong day

1 He's writing letters today, but he usually writes letters on Thursdays.
2 He's playing golf today, but he usually plays on Fridays.
3 He's mowing the lawn today, but he usually mows it on Saturdays.
4 He's washing the car today, but he usually washes it on Sundays.
5 She's doing the shopping today, but she usually does it on Mondays.
6 She's going to her art class today, but she usually goes on Wednesdays.
7 She's doing the ironing today, but she usually does it on Thursdays.
8 She's washing her hair today, but she usually washes it on Fridays.
9 She's playing tennis today, but she usually plays on Saturdays.

3 Zoe and Anna

No fixed answers. Follow example.
► PUPIL 1 *Is she studying English in Greece?*
  PUPIL 2 *No, she isn't. She's studying English in England.*
  PUPIL 1 *Does she like speaking English?*
  PUPIL 2 *Yes, she does.*

4 Let's . . .

1 Let's make some sandwiches.
2 Let's watch television.
3 Let's put on the light.
4 Let's play football.
5 Let's close the window.
6 Let's have something to drink.
7 Let's hurry.
8 Let's look for him.
9 Let's go by bus.
10 Let's ask her.
11 Let's chase Chip.
12 Let's read them in bed.

22 Was Nick ill?

Student's book pages 64–67

Teaching aims

- Past simple of **be: was**, **were**
- Past simple of **have: had**

Vocabulary

composer	headache	sore throat
explorer	inventor	toe
finger	poet	toothache

Presentation

Tell pupils to look at the picture of Nick talking to Mr Blake. They are talking about what happened yesterday.

Read through the text or ask two of the pupils to read the roles.

Make sure they understand the text. Ask them if they think Nick is telling the truth.

Grammar lesson

Ask pupils to look at the presentation and find the verbs in the past tense. Write them on the board.

Review the present tense of the verb **be** with pupils. Write the verb forms on the board. Show them the table in the grammar lesson and explain how it corresponds to the verb **be** in the present. Pupils practise saying the forms.

Do the same for the present and past tenses of the verb **have**.

Explain to pupils that some special expressions are formed with **have** and they must learn these (**have breakfast** etc.)

Read through the presentation again. Ask pupils to make three sentences with the past simple of **be** and three sentences with the past simple of **have**.

1 Where were they yesterday?

[oral   individual]

Aim: past simple of **be** in the third person (singular and plural)

Tell pupils that yesterday the characters in the picture were at the places illustrated. Pupils look at the maze to match the characters to the places. They take turns to say sentences about them in the past tense.

Additional activity: Pupils write the sentences in class or for homework replacing the names of the characters with pronouns.

2 Famous people quiz

[oral   class]

Aim: past simple of **be** in the third person (singular and plural)

Ask pupils to think of famous people from the past. Ask what they were (e.g. scientists, explorers). Write the information in sentences on the board.

Tell pupils to look at the pictures of famous people from the past. Read out the list of occupations and make sure pupils understand what they mean.

Pupils draw lines to match the famous people to the occupations (often more than one have the same occupation) and say sentences like those given as examples.

Additional activities:
- Pupils write their sentences in class or for homework.
- Pupils write out the sentences but substitute the names of the famous people with pronouns.
- Pupils write five sentences about other famous people.

3 Yesterday

[oral / written   individual]

Aim: past simple of **have** in the third person (singular and plural).

Explain that this exercise is about what happened yesterday. Remind pupils of how to make questions and negative sentences with **have** in the past simple. Pupils read the text aloud supplying the correct form of **have**. They write the answers in class or for homework.

Additional activity: In pairs, pupils ask and answer (using short answers) yes / no questions about the sentences.

▶   PUPIL 1   *Did Nick have a temperature yesterday?*
    PUPIL 2   *Yes, he did.*

4 Question time

[oral / written   individual / partner]

Aim: past simple of **have** and **be**

a   Pupils read the questions and write true short answers about themselves.

b   One partner asks the questions and the other one replies with short answers. Then they switch.

Additional activity: Each pupil writes three questions in the same style as those appearing in the exercise (yes / no questions in the simple past with **have** or **be**). He asks another pupil who must reply with short answers. This is repeated five times with different partners.

Answers

1 Where were they yesterday?

(Answers in any order)

Helen was at the shops.
Mick and David were at the sports centre.
Mark was at the cinema.
Jason was at the swimming pool.
Diana was at the circus
Trig was at the sailing club.
Jean and Pat were at the youth club.
Paul was at the library.
Molly and Pam were at the zoo.
Jill and John were at the science museum.

2 Famous people quiz

(Answers in any order)

Agatha Christie was a writer.
Columbus was an explorer.
Beethoven and Mozart were composers.
Charlie Chaplin was a film actor.
Picasso and Van Gogh were artists.
Socrates and Plato were philosophers.
Elvis Presley was a singer.
Homer and Virgil were poets.
Marconi was an inventor.

3 Yesterday

1	have	7	didn't have
2	had	8	have
3	have	9	had, had
4	didn't have	10	had
5	didn't have	11	have
6	had	12	had

4 Question time

a 1 Yes, I was. OR No, I wasn't.
    2 Yes, I was. OR No, I wasn't.
    3 Yes, they were. OR No, they weren't.
    4 Yes, he was. OR No, he wasn't.
    5 Yes, there were. OR No, there weren't.
    6 Yes, there was. OR No, there wasn't.
    7 Yes, I did. OR No, I didn't.
    8 Yes, there was. OR No, there wasn't.
    9 Yes, it was. OR No, it wasn't.
 10 Yes, I did. OR No, I didn't.
 11 Yes, I did. OR No, I didn't.
 12 Yes, I was. OR No, I wasn't.

b Same as **a**

23 Did Trig help?

Student's book pages 68–71

Teaching aims

- Past simple: regular verbs
- **ago**

Vocabulary

bake	empty [vb]	pull up	water [vb]
bury	oil [vb]	smile	watering can
dust [vb]	paint [vb]		

Presentation

Tell pupils that the picture shows Trig a few days ago. Read the text with the pupils. Make sure they understand it.

Ask pupils to pick out all the words in thick type. Write them on the board. Ask pupils what is new or different about the words. Ask them if they know why.

Grammar lesson

Remind pupils of what happens to **be** and **have** when you talk about the past.

Tell them that the past simple of most other verbs is formed with **ed** or **d**. Study the verb tables and examples with the pupils. You could compare these with tables of verbs in the present tense.

Look at the spelling problems and give pupils other verbs to transform into the past simple.

Tell pupils that time expressions with **ago** are sometimes used to indicate the past. Get pupils to practise saying different time expressions with **ago**.

Read through the presentation again. Ask pupils to write five sentences in the past simple.

1 Make lists

[written   individual]

Aim: past simple of regular verbs (form)

Tell pupils to look at the verbs. Explain the meaning of any new vocabulary. Pupils transform the verbs into the past simple and write them in the correct list, according to their spelling.

Tell them that if they are not sure of the answers they can look at the grammar lesson for help.

You can check their answers by asking pupils to read out the lists. Correct their pronunciation.

Additional activity: Pupils write sentences with one verb from each list.

2 A busy week

[oral/written   individual]

Aim: past simple of regular verbs

Tell pupils that the Bells had a busy week last week and that they did many things. Pupils use the words provided to say sentences about what the characters did last week. Then they write in the answers.

Additional activity: Divide the class into two teams. Each team asks the other one yes/no questions about what the Bells did last week.

The teams score one point for a right answer, no points for a wrong answer and they lose a point if they ask a question incorrectly. If the pupils have good memories, they should close their books to play the game. The team with the most points wins.

► TEAM 1   *Did Jenny empty all the rubbish bins?*
  TEAM 2   *No, she didn't. Nick did.* (1 point) OR *Yes, she did.* (0 points)

3 Famous people

[written   individual]

Aim: past simple of regular verbs

a Introduce the idea of famous people from the past (not alive). Ask pupils to look at the pictures and the names of famous people. Encourage pupils to give information about them if they know anything about them. They write the name of the famous person in the correct sentence. Pupils can read their answers out to the class.

b These sentences are about the same famous people as in **a** but they are incorrect. Pupils must read the sentences and then write correct ones. If they cannot remember the facts they should look at **a**. Pupils can read out their answers.

Additional activity: Pupils look at all the sentences in **a** (including the example) except 6 and calculate how many years ago the people died. They make sentences with **ago**.

▶ *Cleopatra died 2,000 years ago.*

4 Did she? Did he?

[oral   partner]

Aim: past simple of regular verbs

In pairs, pupils look at part **a** of Exercise 3 and ask ten questions and give short answers about the famous people.

Additional activity: In two teams, pupils write a questionnaire about any famous people from the past using yes/no questions. They should write at least ten questions. Look at their questions to make sure they are fair.

The other team must answer the questions correctly. The team with the most right answers wins.
▶ TEAM 1   *Did Elvis Presley live in France?*
   TEAM 2   *No, he didn't. He lived in the United States.*

5 What about you?

[oral   individual]

Aim: past simple of regular verbs with **ago**

Review expressions of time and remind pupils of the use of **ago**. Pupils read the questions and give answers about themselves using **ago**, as shown in the example.

Pupils can take turns reading out and answering the questions.

Additional activity: Pupils write out the answers to the questions in complete sentences. Tell them that **be** must be used for some of the answers.
▶ *My birthday was . . . ago.*

Answers

1 Make lists

(Answers in any order)

d	ed	ied	2 × cons + ed
hated	walked	tried	stopped
used	pulled up	tidied	dropped
arrived	watered	carried	shopped
smiled	looked	hurried	planned
danced	filled	buried	clapped
liked	wanted	dried	
		cried	
		studied	
		emptied	

2 A busy week

1 Nick oiled his bicycle.
2 Mrs Bell washed the car.
3 Jenny studied for a Maths test.
4 Mr Bell cleaned the windows.
5 Mrs Bell tidied the bedrooms.
6 Nick emptied all the rubbish bins.
7 Chip buried a smelly bone.
8 Jenny dusted the rooms.
9 Mrs Bell painted the bathroom.
10 Jenny cooked a cheese omelette.
11 Nick worked for a History exam.
12 Mrs Bell baked some cakes.
13 Trig helped in the garden.
14 Trig watered the weeds.

3 Famous people

a 1 John Lennon
    2 Charlie Chaplin
    3 Walt Disney
    4 Leonardo da Vinci
    5 Anna Pavlova
    6 Cleopatra

b 1 She didn't live in France.
      She lived in Egypt.
    2 He didn't die in 1970. He died in 1980.
    3 He didn't create Asterix.
      He created Mickey Mouse.
    4 She didn't live in Spain. She lived in Russia.
    5 She didn't dance in ballets.
      She acted in films.
    6 She didn't die in 1920. She died in 1931.
    7 He didn't paint the 'Mona Lisa'.
      He acted in films.
    8 She didn't die in 1975.
      She died 2,000 years ago.
    9 He didn't live in Russia.
      He lived in England and America.
  10 He didn't direct films.
      He composed many famous songs.
  11 He didn't create Mickey Mouse.
      He painted the 'Mona Lisa'.
  12 He didn't compose songs.
      He created Mickey Mouse.

4 Did she? Did he?

No fixed answers. Follow examples.
> PUPIL 1   *Did Grace Kelly live in Monaco?*
> PUPIL 2   *Yes, she did.*
> PUPIL 2   *Did Walt Disney die in 1519?*
> PUPIL 1   *No, he didn't.*

5 What about you?

No fixed answers. Follow example.
> When was your birthday?
> *About three months ago.* OR *Two weeks ago.*

24 Nick lost his money

Student's book pages 72 – 75

Teaching aim

- Past simple: irregular verbs
  (see Chapter 23 for the past simple of regular verbs)

Vocabulary

build	postcard	sea	sunburn
pay	present	steps	wheel

Presentation

Tell pupils that Nick and Jenny are talking about what happened yesterday. Read through the text or ask two pupils to read the different roles. Ask pupils to pick out the verbs. Write them on the board.

Grammar lesson

Review the past simple of regular verbs with pupils.

Tell pupils to look at the verbs on the board. Ask them to say their base forms. Explain that these and other verbs are exceptions and will have to be learned by heart.

Make pupils practise saying the forms of the verbs on the board.

Read the presentation again. Ask pupils to write three sentences about things they have lost and when they lost them with **ago**. (e.g. *I lost my keys a year ago.*)

1 Pairs

[written   individual]

Aim: past simple of irregular verbs (form)

Review the vocabulary with the pupils. Tell them to look at the verbs and match the base forms to the past simple forms. They must then write them side by side in the correct lists.

Additional activities:
- One pupil says the base form of a verb from the list and another pupil says the past simple form without looking at the book. This can be done with the whole class or as pair work.
- Pupils close their books. You say the base form of one of the verbs and they write down the past simple form.

2 More pairs

[oral   individual / class]

Aim: past simple of irregular verbs (form)

a   Review the vocabulary with the pupils. Pupils draw lines to match up the base forms of verbs to their past simple forms. They read out their pairs of verbs.

b   Follow the instructions for **a**.

Additional activities:
- One pupil says the base form of a verb from the list and another pupil says the past simple form without looking at the book. This can be done with the whole class or as pair work.
- Pupils close their books. You say the base of one of the verbs and they write down the past simple form.

3 A summer holiday

[written   individual]

Aim: past simple of irregular verbs

Ask pupils what they think the Bells did on holiday last year. Pupils read the text and fill in the gaps with verbs in the past simple tense from the list in Exercise 2a. Then they can read out the sentences.

Additional activity: Pupils close their books and say what the Bells did on holiday last year.

4 Trig can do it. Can you?

[written   individual]

Aim: past simple of irregular verbs

Remind pupils of how to make questions in the past simple. Pupils arrange the words in the boxes in order to write questions. Make sure they don't forget capitals and question marks. Then they can read out their questions.

Additional activity: Pupils answer the questions using short or long forms.

5 Your holidays

[oral / written   individual]

Aim: past simple of irregular verbs

a Read through the questions with the pupils. Make sure they understand them. Pupils then write long answers giving information about themselves. If the pupils haven't had a real holiday they must write about an imaginary one.

b Pupils transform their long answers into short ones where possible (questions 3, 6, 10, 12, 14) and say them. A partner could ask the questions.

Additional activity: Pupils write a short paragraph about a holiday they once had or imagine they had.

Answers

1 Pairs

(Answers in any order)

Base form	Past simple
sing	sang
come	came
spend	spent
run	ran
find	found
give	gave
buy	bought
leave	left
pay	paid
build	built
go	went

2 More pairs

a	b
fly, flew	dig, dug
break, broke	drink, drank
fall, fell	think, thought
bring, brought	do, did
write, wrote	tell, told
take, took	stand, stood
sit, sat	be, was
swim, swam	have, had
see, saw	know, knew
eat, ate	begin, began

3 A summer holiday

1	saw	7	took
2	ate	8	got
3	sat	9	fell
4	swam	10	broke
5	made	11	brought
6	wrote		

4 Trig can do it. Can you?

1 Did they sit on the beach?
2 What did they eat?
3 What did Nick and Jenny do on the beach?
4 Did they get sunburned?
5 Did they write many postcards?
6 Did they take photographs?
7 Where did they swim?
8 What did Mr Bell break?
9 Where did he fall?
10 Did he bring home other souvenirs?

5 Your holidays

a Pupils' own answers. Follow examples.
  ▶ Did you go on holiday last year?
    Yes, I went on holiday last year.
  ▶ How many presents or souvenirs did you buy?
    I bought two presents for my best friends, Jane and Sarah.

b Pupils' own answers.
  ▶ *Yes, I did.* OR *No, I didn't.*

25 What's Trig going to do?

Student's book pages 76 – 79

Teaching aim

- **be going to** for future intentions or plans

Vocabulary

author	carpet	pilot	shower
bore	dry [vb]	push	vet

Presentation

Ask pupils to look at the pictures of Trig. Ask them what they think he will do next (or what he is going to do). Tell them that Jenny and Nick are watching Trig and talking about him. Ask pupils to read the text.

Grammar lesson

Use the presentation section text and pictures to show how **going to** expresses what has not happened yet. Ask pupils to look at the verb table and practise saying the different forms: affirmative, negative, question and short answer.

There might be some confusion for pupils between **be going to** + object (present continuous: *I am going to school*) and **be going to** + verb (future intent: *I am going to visit my sister tomorrow*). Be prepared to explain the difference between these two forms.

Ask pupils to write three sentences about what they are going to do tomorrow.

1 What are they going to do?

[written   individual]

Aim: **be going to**

Pupils must make sentences about what the characters are going to do. They read the left hand column to find out about the present situation. They draw lines to match the situations to what the characters intend to do (in the right hand column) and write sentences with **be going to**.

Additional activity: In pairs pupils ask questions and give short answers about the sentences:

▶ PUPIL 1   *Is Mr Bell going to take a cold shower?*
   PUPIL 2   *Yes, he is.*

2 At the weekend

[oral   individual]

Aim: **be going to**

Pupils read the list of activities and say sentences with **be going to** about what they intend to do and what they don't intend to do at the weekend.

Additional activities:

- Pupils write down their answers for homework.
- In pairs, pupils use the prompts to ask and answer five questions.
  ▶ PUPIL 1   *Are you going to visit a friend?*
     PUPIL 2   *Yes I am.* (OR *No, I'm not.*)
- Each pupil makes up three **yes/no** questions about the next holiday and asks five other pupils. They give short answers.

3 Future plans

[oral/written   individual/class]

Aim: **be going to**

The characters in this exercise have made plans for the future. In the left hand column is information about what they like or are good at now and in the right hand column is what they plan to do. Pupils draw lines to match them up. They write sentences about the characters with **be going to**.

Additional activities:

- Based on the sentences in the exercise, the teacher (or a partner) asks pupils what they are going to do in the future and they give short answers.
  ▶ *Are you going to become a pilot?*
     Yes, I am. (OR *No, I'm not.*)
- Each pupils says a sentence about what he or she is going to do in the future.

4 What's going to happen?

[written   individual]

***Aim:* be going to**

The pictures indicate that something is going to happen but has not happened yet. Pupils look at the pictures and write sentences about what is going to happen with **be going to**. Then they can read out their sentences to the class.

Additional activity: Each pupil draws a picture showing a situation in which something is going to happen or someone is going to do something and the class asks questions to find out what is going to happen.

▶   PUPIL   *Is he going to catch the ball?*
      CLASS   *No, he isn't.* (OR *Yes, he is.*)

Answers

1   What are they going to do?

1   He's going to have a drink.
2   She's going to go to bed early.
3   She's going to take some tablets.
4   He's going to watch television.
5   They are going to get some food from the fridge.
6   He's going to have a hot bath.
7   They are going to dry their clothes.
8   He's going to ask his mother.
9   He's going to put on the light.
10   She's going to turn down the radio.
11   He's going to miss the next football match.
12   She's going to look for him in the garden.
13   He's going to telephone the garage.
14   He's going to to see his dentist.

2   At the weekend

Pupils' own answers. Follow examples.
▶   visit a friend
      I'm going to visit a friend.
▶   wash my hair
      I'm not going to wash my hair.

3   Future plans

1   Mark is going to work in a bank.
2   Pam is going to buy a restaurant.
3   Sam is going to become a pilot.
4   Jane is going to become a kindergarten teacher.
5   Scott is going to become a train driver.
6   Sarah is going to study art.
7   Pat is going to study medicine.
8   Ann is going to study computer science.
9   Paul is going to become an author.
10   Bill is going to become a sports teacher.

4   What's going to happen?

1   He's going to pack his suitcase.
2   It's going to rain.
3   She's going to bake a cake.
4   He's going to mow the grass.
5   She's going to drop the books.
6   She's going to fall.
7   He's going to buy (or eat) an ice cream.
8   They're going to play football.
9   It's going to break.
10   They're going to fight.

Tests

Test One [Chapters 1 – 5]

1 Put in the correct long form of the verb **be**.

▶ Chip *is* a good dog.

1 I _____ twelve.
2 Nick and Jenny _____ from Merton.
3 Where _____ Trig from?
4 He _____ not from Athens.
5 _____ you thirteen?

6 John and I _____ twelve.
7 _____ Merton a big town?
8 Yes, it _____ .
9 What _____ your name?
10 My name _____ Susan.

1 mark for each correct answer. Total _____ /10

2 Put the words in order and write correct sentences.

▶ dictionary The an book is Italian . *The book is an Italian dictionary.*

1 flag is It a Greek . _____
2 dictionary a is The red book . _____
3 Greek Nick not and are Jenny . _____
4 is an London city English . _____
5 an big The book is atlas . _____
6 grammar It an English is . _____
7 city a Rome not French is . _____
8 Is Egyptian Carlo an name ? _____
9 is It envelope blue a . _____
10 they German Are coins ? _____

1 mark for each correct answer. Total _____ /10

3 Put the nouns and the verbs in these sentences into plural form.

▶ The man is tall.
   The men are tall.

1 The woman is English.
   _____

2 The baby is big.
   _____

3 The person is Italian.
   _____

4 The bus is red.
   _____

5 Is the bench green?
   _____

6 The coin isn't Greek.
   _____

7 Is the policeman Egyptian?
   _____

8 My foot is cold.
   _____

9 The story is good.
   _____

10 The child isn't happy.
   _____

1 mark for each correct answer. Total _____ /10

4 Read what Jane says and write in the correct pronoun
or possessive adjective from the box.

I	my (×2) ✓
he	his
we	our
you	your
they	their

Hello, ► _my___ name is Jane, ¹_____ am twelve. Meet ²_____ brother. ³_____ name is David. ⁴_____ are from London.

Nick and Jenny are ⁵_____ friends. ⁶_____ are from Merton. Chip is ⁷_____ dog. ⁸_____ is a good dog.

What about you? What is ⁹_____ name? Where are ¹⁰_____ from?

1 mark for each correct answer. Total _____ /10

---

5 Read the sentences. Ring the **'s** and decide if it is a
possessive or a short form. Put a ✓ in the correct box.

		Possessive	Short form
►	My brother('s) name is David.	☑	☐
1	Jenny's my friend.	☐	☐
2	Trig's from Triglon.	☐	☐
3	Is Nick Amanda's brother?	☐	☐
4	Look, it's Chip!	☐	☐
5	It's an old bicycle.	☐	☐
6	This is Tom's house.	☐	☐
7	The hat isn't Amanda's.	☐	☐
8	Nick's twelve.	☐	☐
9	Is the ball Nick's?	☐	☐
10	They are the Jenny's books.	☐	☐

1 mark for each correct answer. Total _____ /10

Total _____ /50

Test Two [Chapters 6 – 10]

1 Write in the correct form of **have got**.

▶ I _haven't got_ (not) a dictionary.

1 Jenny and Nick _____ a new book.

2 It _____ a red cover.

3 We _____(not) a big car.

4 _____ you _____ a cat at home?

5 No, we _____(not).

6 You _____ a funny face.

7 Trig _____(not) big ears.

8 _____ they _____ a piano?

9 Yes, they _____ .

10 I _____(not) a pencil.

2 One of the sentences in each pair is wrong. Read the sentences and put a ✓ in the box beside the one which is correct.

▶ That's Jenny's hat. ☑
  Those are Jenny's hat. ☐

1 This is Nick's ruler. ☐
  Those are Nick's ruler. ☐

2 These are my mother. ☐
  This is my mother. ☐

3 Those are his books. ☐
  This is his books. ☐

4 These shoes are big. ☐
  This shoes are big. ☐

5 Those boy is a good pupil. ☐
  That boy is a good pupil. ☐

6 This is my taxi over there. ☐
  That's my taxi over there. ☐

7 This shirt is green. ☐
  This shirts are green. ☐

8 Those are my sisters over there. ☐
  These are my sisters over there. ☐

9 Those are Trig's sandwich. ☐
  This is Trig's sandwich. ☐

10 Are those your drawings? ☐
   Is that your drawings? ☐

1 mark for each correct answer. Total _____ /10

3 Write **a**, **an** or **some**.

▶ _Some_ bread

1 _____ cheese   6 _____ banana

2 _____ biscuit   7 _____ egg

3 _____ apples   8 _____ crisps

4 _____ sugar   9 _____ jam

5 _____ orange   10 _____ cherries

1 mark for each correct answer. Total _____ /10

4 Write the verbs in brackets () in the present simple.

▶ Jenny and Amanda _play_ (play) the piano.

1 I _____ (watch) television after dinner.

2 Nick and Jenny _____ (walk) to school every morning.

3 Chip _____ (bury) his bones in the garden.

4 Nick _____ (wash) his hands before dinner.

5 No, potatoes _____ (not grow) on trees.

6 We _____ (go) to bed at ten o'clock.

7 No, Jenny _____ (not take) the bus to school.

8 The girls _____ (wear) uniforms.

9 Chip _____ (carry) newspapers in his mouth

10 Trig _____ (like) milk-shakes.

11 Jenny _____ (wake) up at seven o'clock.

12 Fish _____ (swim) under water.

13 Elephants _____ (live) in Africa.

14 Mrs Bell _____ (fry) eggs for breakfast.

15 You _____ (read) comics in bed.

16 Mr Bell _____ (like) steaks.

17 No, Chip _____ (not like) Fluff.

18 Nick _____ (do) his homework after dinner.

19 Five pupils _____ (like) History.

20 We _____ (listen) to music after school.

1 mark for each correct answer. Total _____ /20

Total _____ /50

Test Three [Chapters 11 – 15]

1 Put in **Do**, **Does**, **don't** or **doesn't**.

▶ <u>Does</u> Chip chase the cat?

1 _____ Nick like pizza?

2 No, he _____ .

3 _____ Trig and Chip go to school?

4 No, they _____ .

5 _____ you play football?

6 Yes, I _____ .

7 _____ Jenny buy sweets?

8 Yes, she _____ .

9 _____ we learn English?

10 Yes, we _____ .

1 mark for each correct answer. Total _____ /10

2 Write the words in the correct order to make questions and match them to the correct answers.

▶ do they practise When ?
   <u>When do they practise?</u>   Football.

1 play do you When ?
   _____   At two o'clock.

2 does What time he play ?
   _____   At school.

3 Where they play do ?
   _____   The teacher gives homework.

4 do play What you ?
   _____   On Thursdays.

5 Maths hate Why does Nick ?
   _____   On Saturdays.

2 marks for each correct answer. Total _____ /10

3 Write what your father says to you when you do these things. Sometimes you need to use **Don't**.

► You shout at your sister.

<u>Don't shout at your sister.</u>

1 You don't eat your dinner.

_____

2 You listen to loud music.

_____

3 You don't do your homework.

_____

4 You come home late.

_____

5 You don't practise the piano.

_____

6 You don't write to your grandmother.

_____

7 You don't tidy your room.

_____

8 You don't get up for school.

_____

9 You play football in the house.

_____

10 You don't listen to your mother.

_____

1 mark for each correct answer. Total _____ /10

4 Put a ✓ beside the sentences which are correct.

► There's a shop in Bridge Street. ☑

1 There is a park next to the school. ☐

2 There aren't a cinema. ☐

3 There's a post office in Mill Street. ☐

4 There is many cafés. ☐

5 There isn't a sports centre. ☐

6 Are there a library? ☐

7 Are there many supermarkets? ☐

8 There are many trees in the park. ☐

9 Is there shops next to the bank? ☐

10 There aren't many car parks. ☐

1 mark for each correct answer. Total _____ /10

5 Make true sentences by adding **can** or **can't**.

► Dogs <u>can't</u> talk.

1 Fish _____ run.

2 Spiders _____ play football.

3 Camels _____ walk.

4 Kangaroos _____ jump.

5 Sheep _____ go to school.

6 Parrots _____ fly.

7 Cats _____ play tennis.

8 Penguins _____ catch fish.

9 Horses _____ climb trees.

10 Elephants _____ ride bicycles.

1 mark for each correct answer. Total _____ /10

Total _____ /50

Test Four [Chapters 16 – 20]

1 Complete the sentences by writing the correct words from the list in the present continuous (**be** + **ing**).

talk	chase
write	eat
swim	sleep
sit ✓	play
drink	wash
rain	

▶ Mrs Bell _is sitting_ on the sofa.

1 The weather isn't nice. It _____ .

2 Chip _____ the cat again.

3 Mr Bell and Jenny _____ the car.

4 Jenny _____ a letter to Maria.

5 Trig _____ the chocolate cake.

6 Nick and Tom _____ in the pool.

7 Amanda _____ some lemonade.

8 Nick and his friends _____ football.

9 Mrs Bell _____ on the telephone.

10 Trig _____ in Nick's bed.

1 mark for each correct answer. Total _____ /10

2 Complete the sentences with **can**, **can't**, **must** or **mustn't**.

▶ You _must_ do your homework.

1 _____ I borrow your pen?

2 You _____ make a noise in class.

3 _____ we go to the park?

4 Yes, you _____ .

5 _____ I go to the football match?

6 You _____ learn your verbs.

7 No, you _____ have some money.

8 You _____ fight with your brother.

9 Trig, you _____ pull Chip's tail.

10 _____ I listen to the radio?

1 mark for each correct answer. Total _____ /10

3 Complete the sentences with **me**, **you**, **him**, **her**, **it**, **us**, **you** or **them**.

▶ Jenny can't find her pencils. She is looking for _them_ .

1 Where is Nick? Tom is looking for _____ .

2 I don't know where Nick is. Don't ask _____ .

3 There's Amanda. Ask _____ .

4 We can't find Nick. Help _____ .

5 Nick doesn't like History but Amanda likes _____ .

6 You're late. I can't go with _____ .

7 Trig has got six bananas. He loves eating _____ .

8 Trig and Chip are hiding. Can you find _____ ?

9 Mrs Bell likes tennis and Mr Bell likes _____ too.

10 Nick is talking to Tom and Amanda. He likes talking to _____ .

1 mark for each correct answer. Total _____ /10

4 Write the sentences with the words in brackets ().

▶ I clean my room. (sometimes)
I sometimes clean my room.

1 Nick is late for school. (often)
_____

2 I go to the dentist's. (twice a year)
_____

3 Trig and Chip are hungry. (always)
_____

4 Jenny plays the piano. (every evening)
_____

5 You are a good pupil. (usually)
_____

6 We walk to school. (every morning)
_____

7 Nick makes his bed. (never)
_____

8 Mr Bell reads the paper on the train. (always)
_____

9 Amanda writes to her pen friend. (once a month)
_____

10 I am angry. (rarely)
_____

1 mark for each correct answer. Total _____ /10

5 Complete the sentences with **some**, **any**, **how much** or **how many**.

Nick and Jenny are making a pizza for dinner.

JENNY   We need ▶ *Some* _____ flour, 1 _____ salt and
        2 _____ tomatoes.

NICK   We haven't got 3 _____ tomatoes. 4 _____ do we need?

JENNY   Five or six. Have we got 5 _____ cheese?

NICK   6 _____ do we need?

JENNY   Not much. We also need 7 _____ olives and 8 _____ chocolate.

NICK   Chocolate? We haven't got 9 _____ chocolate. 10 _____
        do we need?

JENNY   We need a big bar of chocolate for me to eat right now!

1 mark for each correct answer. Total _____ /10

| Total _____ /50 |

Test Five [Chapters 21 – 25]

1 Write the verbs in present continuous (I am eating . . .) or present simple form (I eat . . .).

▶ Look! Nick *is playing* _____ (play) football.

1 Nick and Jenny usually _____ (walk) to school.

2 Be quiet! Mr Bell _____ (sleep) now.

3 Mrs Bell _____ (talk) to Mrs Langton.

4 I can't help now. I _____ (write) a letter.

5 Jenny _____ (play) tennis once a week.

6 Mr Bell usually _____ (mow) the lawn on Saturdays.

7 Amanda's not here. She _____ (help) with the school play.

8 Mrs Bell is busy at the moment. She _____ (make) dinner.

9 Nick _____ (do) his homework every day.

10 Jenny _____ (like) school.

1 mark for each correct answer. Total _____ /10

---

2 Cross out the verb which is wrong.

▶ Nick has/had a cold yesterday.

1 Chip was/were a good dog last week.

2 Mr Bell didn't had/didn't have his keys yesterday.

3 Mrs Bell wasn't/weren't home last week.

4 Jenny was/had in Scotland last summer.

5 Trig didn't have/wasn't supper last night.

6 Last year, Jenny was/had ten years old.

7 Amanda wasn't/hadn't at school last week.

8 Jenny and Nick was/were in London last weekend.

9 Last week Jenny had/was a birthday party.

10 The Bells was/were at Tom's football match last week.

1 mark for each correct answer. Total _____ /10

3 Put the verbs from the box in the past simple and complete the sentences.

bake	help ✓	water	paint
pull	bury	study	dance
empty	tidy	walk	

Yesterday . . .

▶ Trig *helped* _____ Mrs Bell do the washing up.

1 Jenny _____ her room.

2 Mr Bell _____ the flowers.

3 Mrs Bell _____ a cake.

4 Nick _____ French verbs.

5 Chip _____ some bones in the garden.

6 Amanda _____ in the school play.

7 Mr Bell _____ up the weeds in the garden.

8 Jenny _____ a picture.

9 Nick _____ the rubbish bins.

10 Amanda and Jenny _____ to the park.

1 mark for each correct answer. Total _____ /10

4 Write the past simple of these verbs.

▶ make *made*   7 give _____   14 begin _____

1 think _____   8 sing _____   15 think _____

2 take _____   9 go _____   16 know _____

3 drink _____   10 see _____   17 tell _____

4 find _____   11 run _____   18 stand _____

5 write _____   12 break _____   19 do _____

6 buy _____   13 fly _____   20 have _____

½ mark for each correct answer. Total _____ **/10**

5 Make sentences about what they intend to do this weekend with **be going to**.

▶ Jenny - wash her hair
Jenny is going to wash her hair.

1 Mr and Mrs Bell - play tennis

2 Trig - sleep

3 Amanda - shop in London

4 Chip - chase Fuff

5 Tom - run in the park

6 Nick - buy some comic books

7 Jenny - watch television

8 Mr Todd - fix his car

9 Mr and Mrs Langton - visit their uncle

10 Mr and Mrs Bell - paint the kitchen

1 mark for each correct answer. Total _____ **/10**

Total _____ /50

Answer key to tests

Test One

1

1	am	6	are
2	are	7	Is
3	is	8	is
4	is	9	is
5	Are	10	is

2

1 It is a Greek flag.
2 The red book is a dictionary.
3 Nick and Jenny are not Greek.
4 London is an English city.
5 The big book is an atlas.
6 It is an English grammar.
7 Rome is not a French city.
8 Is Carlo an Egyptian name?
9 It is a blue envelope.
10 Are they German coins?

3

1 The women are English.
2 The babies are big.
3 The people are Italian.
4 The buses are red.
5 Are the benches green?
6 The coins aren't Greek.
7 Are the policemen Egyptian?
8 My feet are cold.
9 The stories are good.
10 The children aren't happy.

4

1	I	6	They
2	my	7	their
3	His	8	He
4	We	9	your
5	our	10	you

5

		Possesive	Short form
1	Jenny's my friend.	☐	☑
2	Trig's from Triglon.	☐	☑
3	Is Nick Amanda's brother?	☑	☐
4	Look, it's Chip!	☐	☑
5	It's an old bicycle.	☐	☑
6	This is Tom's house.	☑	☐
7	The hat isn't Amanda's.	☑	☐
8	Nick's twelve.	☐	☑
9	Is the ball Nick's?	☑	☐
10	They are the Jenny's books.	☑	☐

Test Two

1

1	have got	6	have got
2	has got	7	hasn't got
3	haven't got	8	Have . . . got
4	Have . . . got	9	have
5	haven't	10	haven't got

2

1	This is Nick's ruler.	☑
	Those are Nick's ruler.	☐
2	These are my mother.	☐
	This is my mother.	☑
3	Those are his books.	☑
	This is his books.	☐
4	These shoes are big.	☑
	This shoes are big.	☐
5	Those boy is a good pupil.	☐
	That boy is a good pupil.	☑
6	This is my taxi over there.	☐
	That's my taxi over there.	☑
7	This shirt is green.	☑
	This shirts are green.	☐
8	Those are my sisters over there.	☑
	These are my sisters over there.	☐
9	Those are Trig's sandwich.	☐
	This is Trig's sandwich.	☑
10	Are those your drawings?	☑
	Is that your drawings?	☐

3

1	some	6	a
2	a	7	an
3	some	8	some
4	some	9	some
5	an	10	some

4

1	watch	11	wakes
2	walk	12	swim
3	buries	13	live
4	washes	14	fries
5	don't grow	15	read
6	go	16	likes
7	doesn't take	17	doesn't like
8	wear	18	does
9	carries	19	like
10	likes	20	listen

Test Three

1

1	Does	6	do
2	doesn't	7	Does
3	Do	8	does
4	don't	9	Do
5	Do	10	do

2

1 When do you play? On Saturdays.
2 What time does he play? At two o'clock.
3 Where do they play? At school.
4 What do you play? Football.
5 Why does Nick hate Maths? The teacher gives homework.

3

1 Eat your dinner.
2 Don't listen to loud music.
3 Do your homework.
4 Don't come home late.
5 Practise the piano.
6 Write to your grandmother.
7 Tidy your room.
8 Get up for school.
9 Don't play football in the house.
10 Listen to your mother.

4

1	There is a park next to the school. ☑
2	There aren't a cinema. ☐
3	There's a post office in Mill Street. ☑
4	There is many cafés. ☐
5	There isn't a sports centre. ☑
6	Are there a library? ☐
7	Are there many supermarkets? ☑
8	There are many trees in the park. ☑
9	Is there shops next to the bank? ☐
10	There aren't many car parks. ☑

5

1	can't	6	can
2	can't	7	can't
3	can	8	can
4	can	9	can't
5	can't	10	can't

Test Four

1

1	is raining	6	are swimming
2	is chasing	7	is drinking
3	are washing	8	are playing
4	is writing	9	is talking
5	is eating	10	is sleeping

2

1	Can	6	must
2	mustn't	7	can't
3	Can	8	mustn't
4	can	9	mustn't
5	Can	10	Can

3

1	him	6	you
2	me	7	them
3	her	8	them
4	us	9	it
5	it	10	them

4

1 Nick is often late for school.
2 I go to the dentist's twice a year.
3 Trig and Chip are always hungry.
4 Jenny plays the piano every evening.
5 You are usually a good pupil.
6 We walk to school every morning.
7 Nick never makes his bed.
8 Mr Bell always reads the paper on the train.
9 Amanda writes to her pen friend once a month.
10 I am rarely angry.

5

1	some	6	How much
2	some	7	some
3	any	8	some
4	How many	9	any
5	any/some	10	How much

Test Five

1

1	walk	6	mows
2	is sleeping	7	is helping
3	is talking	8	is making
4	am writing	9	does
5	plays	10	likes

2

1	was	6	was
2	didn't have	7	wasn't
3	wasn't	8	were
4	was	9	had
5	didn't have	10	were

3

1	tidied	6	danced
2	watered	7	pulled
3	baked	8	painted
4	studied	9	emptied
5	buried	10	walked

4

1	thought	11	ran
2	took	12	broke
3	drank	13	flew
4	found	14	began
5	wrote	15	thought
6	bought	16	knew
7	gave	17	told
8	sang	18	stood
9	went	19	did
10	saw	20	had

5

1 Mr and Mrs Bell are going to play tennis.
2 Trig is going to sleep.
3 Amanda is going to shop in London.
4 Chip is going to chase Fluff.
5 Tom is going to run in the park.
6 Nick is going to buy some comic books.
7 Jenny is going to watch television.
8 Mr Todd is going to fix his car.
9 Mr and Mrs Langton are going to visit their uncle.
10 Mr and Mrs Bell are going to paint the kitchen.

Oxford University Press
Great Clarendon Street, Oxford OX2 6DP

Oxford New York
Athens Auckland Bangkok Bogotá Buenos Aires
Cape Town Chennai Dar es Salaam Delhi
Florence Hong Kong Istanbul Karachi Kolkata
Kuala Lumpur Madrid Melbourne Mexico City
Mumbai Nairobi Paris São Paulo Shanghai
Singapore Taipei Tokyo Toronto Warsaw

and associated companies in
Berlin Ibadan

OXFORD AND OXFORD ENGLISH
are trade marks of Oxford University Press.

ISBN 0 19 431450 2

Typeset in Baskerville by Tradespools Ltd, Frome, Somerset
Printed in China